RAGGEDY TO RICHES

Raggedy to Riches

Getting Rich Off Raggedy Houses

Elvin Ames

Contents

Dedication

"Raggedy to Riches" is dedicated to my beautiful daughter. Your radiant spirit brightens my world, and in your laughter and innocence, I find constant inspiration. This book is a tribute to the boundless dreams and limitless potential that reside within you. May its words guide you and offer encouragement as you carve your own path in life.

To my beloved wife, Lady Carla, your unwavering love and belief in my dreams keep me grounded. Through every high and low, your presence has been a beacon of strength and support. This book stands as a testament to our enduring partnership, an ode to the shared dreams we've nurtured and the milestones we've celebrated together.

To my remarkable mother, Doreen, your love, wisdom, and steadfast support have been my guiding stars. You've nurtured my dreams and instilled in me the confidence to chase them fearlessly. This book is a tribute to your profound influence on my life.

To my intelligent siblings, Sebastian (affectionately known as Patrick), Patricia, and Katrina, our shared experiences and unbreakable bond have shaped the stories I long to tell. Each of you has added unique perspectives and characters to my narrative canvas. This dedication celebrates our intertwined lives and the strength we find in one another.

To my father, Elvin Ames Sr., thank you for always stressing the value of education and planning for the future.

To my grandmother, Justine Burke, your unwavering determination and resilience continue to inspire me. Deep within, I carry the lessons you imparted—the importance of perseverance and unwavering faith. To my aunts Pauline, Kathleen, Sandra, and Wendy, and my uncles Gravy and Simeon, your wisdom and presence have been sources of joy and strength throughout my journey.

I honor in reverence those who have left this earthly realm, leaving behind cherished memories. Rest in peace, Auntie Maria Burke and Auntie Annie Burke.

To my childhood best friend, Kym Lucas of Barbados, rest in peace. World Peace Posse forever—the name of our hip-hop dance group in the 1990s. WPP!

To Poetic the Grym Reaper, also known as Anthony Ian Berkeley, I'm still your Sharpshooter, brother. Your daughter has become an amazing rapper, just like her dad. Though you've left this world, your spirit remains forever in my heart. This dedication is a testament to your lasting impact on my life.

To my best friend Antwan Jackson from Newark, rest in peace, brother. We love and miss you. I could never have built this business without you—you'll always be my right-hand commander, my right-hand man.

I am deeply humbled by the love, support, and memories that have shaped me into the storyteller I am today. With each stroke of the pen, I embark on a journey, knowing that the chapters ahead will hold both joys and sorrows, victories and trials. Yet, it is in the telling of this tale that I hope to touch hearts, ignite creative imagination, and kindle the entrepreneurial spirit in others.

THE FINANCIAL 4 PLEX™

CHAPTER 1

THE FINANCIAL 4 PLEX™: THE SUCKER, THE BUSTER, THE HUSTLER, THE BALLER

A BRIEF OVERVIEW

When my brother and I bought our first property, a 4-plex (also known as a 4-unit or 4-family house), we purchased it from an experienced landlord who had owned it for many years. We soon realized that each of the four units housed a different type of tenant, what I call the "THE FINANCIAL 4 PLEX™": The Sucker, The Buster, The Hustler, and The Baller. Let me explain:

1. **The Sucker**: This tenant was on Section 8, draining the financial system like a vampire. They live in fear of wealth—trapped in poverty with no path to economic mobility. Any attempt to rise out of their financial trap is met with the removal of their safety net, leaving them stuck.
2. **The Buster**: A hardworking employee, the Buster busts their ass from 9 to 5, living paycheck to paycheck. Trapped in a cycle of financial obligations,

they see much of their earnings vanish through taxes and deductions they barely understand.

3. **The Hustler**: The self-employed tenant running their own business, the Hustler faces the constant challenges of financial instability. Despite their entrepreneurial spirit, they're frequently knocked off course by the ever-changing political, economic, and social environments.

4. **The Baller**: The owner-occupied landlord, or Baller, who controls the cash flow of the 4-plex. They have mastered the Perpetual Wealth Cycle, allowing them to live without ever having to work again. They leverage income, depreciation, equity, appreciation, and control of their assets to build lasting wealth.

Let's dive deeper into each type of tenant.

The Sucker

The Sucker lives in fear of wealth, relying heavily on government assistance and trapped in a system that discourages any attempt at financial growth. Whether it's a person stuck on Section 8 or someone avoiding a career because the real world seems too daunting, the Sucker is imprisoned by the very safety net that's supposed to help. Once they try to escape, that support is yanked away, keeping them stuck in poverty.

Society views them as helpless, but in reality, they are financial prisoners. The Sucker may look like a taker, but the system is designed to keep them from realizing their full potential. Don't be a Sucker!

Statistics show that 19% of Americans live below the

poverty line, relying heavily on government assistance programs and struggling to achieve financial independence.

The Buster

The Buster works a typical 9-to-5 job, barely scraping by and living paycheck to paycheck. They are the backbone of American society but find themselves losing 40% of their income to taxes and deductions. Despite their hard work, they remain stuck in a cycle of debt and financial uncertainty.

Most Busters have no idea where a significant portion of their income goes. For example, could you explain these deductions?

- FED
- FICA
- SS SOCSEC
- FIT
- SIT
- OASDI

These abbreviations represent a portion of the Buster's earnings, funneled into government programs, while they struggle to stay afloat. Meanwhile, the wealthy get tax breaks, and the very poor receive assistance, but the Buster is left waiting for a possible tax refund to maybe fix their car or take a short vacation. Don't die a Buster!

Research reveals that 53% of Americans live paycheck to paycheck, vulnerable to financial emergencies and struggling to cover basic expenses.

The Hustler

Society glamorizes the Hustler: the go-getter with a string of business ventures, always chasing the next big opportunity. They've left behind the security of a steady paycheck to be their own boss, but they often find themselves bouncing from boom to bust. Hustlers face a constant roller coaster of political, economic, and social challenges that hinder long-term success.

While the Hustler has the qualities necessary for success—drive, passion, and courage—they are often trapped by market forces beyond their control. Whether it's investing in real estate just before a market crash or jumping into the latest business trend at the wrong time, Hustlers can't seem to break free from the cycle of near-misses and setbacks.

Statistics show that around 50% of small businesses fail within five years, often due to cash flow issues, competition, and market volatility. Don't get stuck as a Hustler!

The Baller

The term "Baller" is a metaphor for making money work for you, rather than the other way around. In this context, tenants pay the owner's mortgage, allowing the owner to live in their property for free. Who wouldn't want someone else to cover 50% of their paycheck to pay down your mortgage, while the property appreciates and builds equity each month as the principal shrinks? Here's the truth about being a Baller: you don't have to be a millionaire to achieve this status. It's all based on the Perpetual Wealth Cycle, which means you can support your lifestyle without additional effort or work.

To reach this level, you need time or money. Some people, like Busters, achieve it after retirement by relying on pensions and Social Security. They might even have to move to a cheaper country, like Mexico, to cover their expenses, but they no longer need to work. The downside for Busters is that they had to toil away at their job for 20-30 years to get those benefits. If their company goes bankrupt, their pension is at risk. If the stock market crashes, their 401(k) is at risk. And with Social Security being used to fund needless wars, that safety net is also in jeopardy.

There's another way to reach Baller status: through hustling. By accumulating assets, you can let the cash flow from those assets pay for your lifestyle. This shortcut to Baller status works better than waiting because of the snowball effect. Assets provide cash flow, which improves your profit and loss statement and balance sheet, allowing you to borrow more funds to acquire more assets. The cycle continues, growing your wealth faster.

The Baller mindset represents the pinnacle of financial success. You've hustled your way to the top, realizing that endless grinding isn't the path to true wealth. Your assets work for you, funding the lifestyle you want without constant effort. You've discovered a fundamental truth that the wealthy have always known: wealth generates more wealth, and once you have it, managing it carefully ensures its preservation. You've achieved what many aspire to but few attain, even as others criticize the very success they secretly desire.

However, being a Baller comes with challenges. You must protect your wealth by creating trusts and foundations to shelter your assets from taxes, lobbying Congress to maintain your advantage, and safeguarding your interests. Some Ballers even buy influence with Supreme Court judges and pay for their children's education or family homes. Who wouldn't want to own a corrupt judge? As a Baller, you're the embodiment of the American Dream, turning ambition into reality, and everyone admires you for it.

Around 8.8% of Americans are millionaires, and while not all are Ballers, many are close. According to a Federal Reserve report, the wealthiest 1% of Americans own more wealth than the bottom 90% combined, illustrating the concentrated financial power of Ballers. You, too, can become a Baller!

So, where do you stand? What's your mindset?

Do you identify with the Sucker, fearing wealth and trapped in financial struggle? Or are you a Buster, working tirelessly but unable to break free from paycheck-to-paycheck living? Maybe you're a Hustler, navigating the ups and downs of entrepreneurship with determination. Or are you already a Baller, enjoying the fruits of your hard work?

Wherever you are, with the right mindset, learning, dedication, and action, you can rise to the top of THE FINANCIAL 4 PLEX™!

CHAPTER 2

THE RAG MAN

How do you transition from rags to riches, from the basement to the penthouse? The key lies in adopting the mindset of the Rag Man or Rag Woman. You must think beyond conventional boundaries and take bold action. This book will provide you with invaluable knowledge and wisdom that took me a lifetime to acquire. However, remember that without putting this knowledge into action, you might find yourself stuck in the same place a year from now, still wondering why you're not progressing.

When I first ventured into real estate investing, the prevailing advice from so-called gurus was to plaster "WE BUY HOUSES" signs with our phone numbers everywhere. Naturally, everyone followed suit, leading to a flood of identical signs across America. Sellers couldn't distinguish between investors, making it challenging to stand out. I also put up these signs but soon noticed that most calls were from people whose homes were already listed with agents but not selling quickly. These homes were often in good condition, and the sellers expected market value, leaving no profit margin for me as an investor.

I decided to pivot. I focused solely on "RAGGEDY

HOUSES" and created the domain www.webuyraggedyhous es.com to attract sellers of properties in need of Tender Loving Care (TLC). Our iconic 1-800-RAG-BUGG beetle, adorned with a mascot named Ragman, became a symbol of our unique approach, which helped us establish a reputation in the industry.

Side Story: When my brother Sebastian and I first ventured into door-knocking with distressed sellers, we adopted a simple strategy: I wore a suit to project a professional image, and we drove around in an unassuming car. However, we quickly faced two significant hurdles:

- *First, many people were hesitant to open their doors to someone in formal attire. They often mistook me for a Jehovah's Witness or assumed I was selling something unwanted, perhaps even suspecting me of being a government official.*
- *Second, even if we managed to engage them, they often questioned our credibility, doubting whether we had the financial capacity to follow through on our promises.*

Reflecting on these challenges, I asked myself: who do people readily welcome at their doorsteps, and who do they trust to deliver? It dawned on me that in 2003, certain uniformed professionals enjoyed instant trust and access. Postmen in their distinctive white and blue uniforms, UPS drivers in their reliable brown attire, meter readers from utility companies, and familiar faces from FedEx and DHL all had a level of trust and acceptance that we lacked.

With this insight, we decided to rebrand. We donned company-branded red shirts featuring our logo and transformed our vehicle into a vibrant, branded VW Beetle. You could even reach us at the memorable number 1-800-RAG-BUGG.

The impact was immediate: more people welcomed us at their doors, and the question of our financial capability never arose again. It seemed that our matching attire and vehicle signaled reliability and trustworthiness, alleviating any doubts about our ability to deliver on our promises.

A Philosophy and Foundation: Who Is the Rag Man?

Who is the Rag Man? The Rag Man represents resilience, determination, and unconventional thinking. He sees potential where others see only neglect and despair. Despite being labeled as a bottom-feeder or vulture by society, the Rag Man thrives on transforming overlooked properties into valuable assets. Dressed in a scruffy t-shirt, worn jeans, and rugged boots, he embodies the gritty, hands-on approach essential for success in house flipping. While suits may not be suitable for this kind of work, the Rag Man's mindset is a powerful tool for turning hidden opportunities into wealth.

Despite facing judgment and skepticism, the Rag Man remains steadfast in his purpose. He tackles challenges head-on, addressing the neglected houses and situations that others lack the expertise to handle.

"I am the Rag Man!" he declares. "If you're wise, you'll become a Rag Man or Rag Woman, too. What some consider junk is treasure to others. We turn rags into riches."

This philosophy is embodied by our company's flagship brand, www.WeBuyRaggedyHouses.com. Our mission goes beyond mere development; we aim to **ReVelop**—to renovate, reposition, resuscitate, rehabilitate, and revitalize. Explore upcoming franchise opportunities at www.revelopers.com.

. . .

The Rag Man's ideology is encapsulated in his name:

- **(R)esurrecting Opportunities:** The Rag Man thrives in the underbelly of the market, salvaging hidden wealth where others fear to tread, much like a vulture resurrecting overlooked opportunities from the dead.
- **(A)daptive Wealth Creation:** Rejecting the traditional grind for monetary gain, the Rag Man harnesses the power of passive income, adapting his approach to make money work for him.
- **(G)enius Unconventionality:** Embracing unconventional thinking, the Rag Man discovers treasures hidden from the conventional eye through his unique and ingenious approach.
- **(M)aster of Truth:** Often mistaken for rudeness, the Rag Man's bluntness stems from a commitment to truth, fearlessly addressing uncomfortable realities that others avoid.
- **(A)gile Protector:** Like a vigilant shark guarding its territory, the Rag Man navigates the real estate waters with agility and purpose, fiercely protecting his interests.
- **(N)ifty Frugality:** With a disdain for wasteful spending, the Rag Man maximizes the value of every dollar, using clever frugality as a strategic pathway to wealth creation.

Fun Fact! The original Rag Man 1.0 mascot was designed to resemble a Great Depression-era vagrant. However, faced with resistance from billboard companies, we developed Rag Man 2.0—a carpenter-inspired character—to overcome this obstacle.

. . .

Understanding real estate and its role in building your wealth is crucial. I'm not just talking about quick profits from flipping homes, though that can be part of your overall strategy. Different types of real estate can help you diversify your portfolio and create multiple streams of income. This way, if one investment—say, a flipped home—encounters a setback, like burning down, you have other income sources to offset the loss.

But why real estate? What makes property ownership the key to achieving real, meaningful, and tangible success?

THE IMPORTANCE OF REAL ESTATE

Real estate investing offers unique advantages, summarized in the acronym **I.D.E.A.L.** Here's a breakdown of each component:

- **Income:** Real estate provides a consistent flow of earnings through rental income or profits from strategic buying and selling. This steady income allows you to sustain your investments, cover expenses, and save for the future without being tied to a traditional job.
- **Depreciation:** Property owners benefit from depreciation, a hidden tax deduction that reduces taxable income, enabling you to retain more earnings annually and pay less in taxes. These deductions cover expenses incurred during the acquisition and enhancement of the property, spread over its lifespan.
- **Equity:** Equity is the difference between what you owe on the property (mortgage, taxes, lines of credit, etc.) and its current value. For example, if you buy a $100,000 home and put down $10,000, you have 10% equity. However, until the mortgage is fully paid off, the bank technically retains underlying ownership.

This highlights the notion that ownership is somewhat illusory until all debts are settled.

- **Appreciation:** Appreciation refers to the increase in property value over time. For instance, if you purchase a house for $100,000 and its value rises to $110,000 within a year, your property has appreciated by 10% without any additional effort on your part.
- **Leverage:** Leveraging involves using other people's money (OPM), often through bank financing, to control a larger asset with a smaller investment. This allows investors to amplify their returns. For example, if you put down $10,000 to purchase a $100,000 property, you control the asset for just 10% of its value. In contrast, investing the same amount in stocks limits returns to the initial investment, making leveraging real estate potentially more lucrative.

This leverage is typically facilitated through a mortgage, which involves two key documents: a **note** and a **mortgage**. A note is an IOU—a legal contract between you and the lender that outlines repayment terms. A mortgage is what you pledge to the lender, usually recorded as a lien on the property's title. This lien indicates that the lender must be paid off before the property can be sold, making the mortgage a form of "dead pledge," derived from the French words *mort* (dead) and *gage* (pledge).

CHAPTER 3

RAGGEDY BEGINNINGS

Once upon a time in the sunny paradise of Barbados, my family lived in what I affectionately call a "government-sponsored vacation spot." Let me clarify: we weren't exactly rolling in dough. Our house was more of a government hand-me-down than a dream home, and our savings were about as nonexistent as a unicorn at a petting zoo.

Picture this: it's a Sunday morning, and we're getting all dressed up for church. My aunts are on a mission, scouring every nook and cranny for loose change to toss into the offering plate at our Seventh-Day Adventist service. Money was tighter than my grandma's knitting stitches, but we were determined to make our contribution.

So, there we were, trekking two miles to the church under the scorching Caribbean sun, sweat pouring down our brows like we were trying to outdo Niagara Falls. Just when we thought we couldn't sweat any more, the pastor rolls in, shining in his limo, looking like he just stepped out of a magazine ad for "Pastors Gone Wild."

Imagine this: the church is packed to the rafters, fans whirring as if auditioning for the next summer blockbuster, and the heat so oppressive you could cut it with a butter knife. We're all fanning ourselves like we're in "Sweltering Sundays: The Musical."

Then, like clockwork, the pastor rings the bell for the offering. Round one: it's for his vacation. My aunts reluctantly dig into their pockets, scraping together every last penny like they're playing a game of find-the-lost-treasure.

But wait, it gets better! Round two: now it's for his wife's vacation. My aunts start to panic, beads of sweat racing down their foreheads as if in a competition. Somehow, they manage to scrounge up a few more coins to toss in.

And just when we think it's safe to breathe again, the pastor drops the bombshell: round three! This time, it's for his daughter's school trip to Granada. My aunts look ready to stage a protest, having given their last penny—and then some.

At that moment, I turned to my auntie Pauline and said, "Don't ever bring me here again." And let me tell you, I meant it. From that day forward, you wouldn't catch me inside a church unless it was for a special occasion like a baptism, funeral, or wedding.

Yet, despite the absurdity of it all, I learned something invaluable that day. Even a thirteen-year-old kid with dyslexia can see through the lies more clearly than the so-called "grown-ups" around him. And make no mistake, there are many liars out there, especially regarding tradition, religion, and culture. We want to b-e-l-i-e-v-e, but between the Be and the Ve is the word Lie!

I traded in my Sunday sermons for a job at the local supermarket, and you know what? Bagging groceries was far more fulfilling than listening to a pastor preach about fire and brimstone. As I grew older, I realized something else: society has a funny way of valuing all the wrong things.

In Barbados, education focused heavily on English and math,

despite our awareness of multiple intelligences since the 1980s. Not sure what that means? Let me break it down:

- **Linguistic Intelligence**: While English is important, it's just one facet of intelligence. Linguistic intelligence encompasses a range of spoken and written languages.
- **Logical-Mathematical Intelligence**: Numbers are useful, but they don't define intelligence. Without logic guiding your analysis, math can only take you so far.
- **Spatial Intelligence**: Have you ever met someone who navigates a maze with ease? That's spatial intelligence in action.
- **Musical Intelligence**: Some people have an incredible ear for music, which can empower them in remarkable ways.
- **Bodily-Kinesthetic Intelligence**: This relates to dancers, athletes, and anyone with impressive physical skills and body awareness.
- **Interpersonal Intelligence**: The ability to understand and connect with others is a valuable skill.
- **Intrapersonal Intelligence**: And let's not overlook self-awareness.

So, while Barbados emphasized English and math, there's a whole world of intelligence waiting to be explored.

Coming to America

Fast forward a few years, and at 17, I'm packing my bags for America. My father got a teaching job at Rikers Island in NYC, and my mom, who was an English teacher, had moved to America to work as a nanny and private tutor for wealthy kids in

Manhattan. They had outgrown Barbados, which, although rich in talent, lacked the economic opportunities found in the USA.

I knew little about America and didn't choose to come here. I arrived as a teenager in 1993, but in hindsight, it was the best decision my parents ever made for me—though it took me a few years to realize it.

Side Story: When my mother mentioned she lived off Broadway, I was ecstatic. I envisioned myself mingling with Broadway stars and soaking in the glitz and glamour of the theater scene. As I bid farewell to Barbados, I boasted to my friends about my imminent stardom, unable to contain my excitement.

Upon landing at JFK Airport, I was filled with anticipation. My uncle Gravy whisked me away, and as we drove through the streets, I eagerly searched for signs of the illustrious Broadway. However, what I encountered was far from the dazzling lights and grand theaters I had imagined. Instead, we passed dilapidated brownstones and neglected streets.

"Mom, is this Broadway?" I asked, my voice tinged with concern. My mother, puzzled, assured me that it was. Confusion clouded my thoughts as we turned onto Chauncey Street, nestled between Broadway and Rockaway. "This can't be Broadway!" I protested, my Bajan accent thickening with incredulity.

Amidst my bewilderment, my mother and uncle exchanged amused glances. "Son," my mother chuckled, "this is Chauncey Street, off Broadway and Rockaway, in Brownsville, Brooklyn."

My heart sank as I grasped the stark reality. "You mean there's more than one Broadway?" I exclaimed, feeling utterly deceived.

"Yes," my mother replied with a chuckle, "the Broadway you're thinking of is in Manhattan. We can't afford to live there!"

As we parked in front of what resembled a set from a dystopian movie, my disappointment was palpable. My dreams of

Broadway fame were shattered by the harsh truth of our budgetary constraints. I was not amused.

Crimeville, Crooklyn: Better Known as Brownsville, Brooklyn

It didn't take long for me to realize I had moved to the murder capital of NYC at the time: Brownsville, Brooklyn. To put it plainly, I joined the Marines a year later at 18 to escape Brooklyn. Joining the U.S. Marines, particularly the infantry—the toughest military branch in America and the tip of the spear in military engagements—was far easier than living in that hell-hole locals called Crimeville, Crooklyn.

I came to America at 17, already having worked for three years after graduating high school at 14 in Barbados, which was common. I wasn't a genius; my mother, unsure of what to do with me, took me to the Board of Education. They told her I needed to take a test to determine my grade placement.

I remember sitting on a makeshift trailer with other kids, receiving a piece of paper. I finished the test in about ten minutes and raised my hand to indicate I was done. The test administrator looked stunned. She waved me forward and took my multiple-choice paper.

She pulled out a card with holes punched in it and positioned it over my paper. All her holes lined up perfectly with my black dots. She looked up at me, then back at the paper, and asked if I had cheated. Bewildered, I replied that I hadn't; the test was easy. I had done all that work when I was 13 or 14 before I graduated.

She asked how old I was when I graduated. I told her I was 14 in Barbados. She asked another kid in the trailer to watch the room to prevent cheating and then led me outside to a payphone (this was 1993; no one had cell phones, and pagers were not widespread yet). She asked me to call my mother and handed the phone to her. All I remember the lady saying to my mother was, "He is in the wrong place!" The next day, my mother took my Barbados high school diploma and transcript to a degree evaluation office in Manhattan, and I was placed in New York Technical College in downtown Brooklyn.

My Downward Slide

Eventually, I fell in with a rough crowd, not by choice but by proximity. New York was different from L.A., where large gangs thrived. In New York, we had crews—mostly groups of wannabe thugs and hoodlums from a few blocks or project buildings in the same vicinity.

My block on Chauncey, between Broadway and Rockaway by the J train, was called the **Crime Kings**! The crews formed mainly out of the need for protection. There were gangs like the Duces, Latin Kings, and Decepticons, but they didn't hold much sway over the neighborhood crews controlling the blocks and checking newcomers.

One night, a few of us went to a club around the corner, and when Method Man's song "Pain" started playing, it typically led to some shoving on the dance floor. Someone pushed me into a Puerto Rican kid from the projects up the hill. He turned around and pushed me back, prompting me to punch him in the face. He fell to the ground, and I began hitting him while standing over him.

Suddenly, several pairs of Timberland boots kicked me in the face. Before I knew it, I was rolling on the ground, getting jumped by four other guys. My crew wasn't around they had stepped outside earlier following some girls they were trying to *holla at*, leaving me alone on the dance floor.

.   .   .

__A quick note:__ The beating wasn't as bad as it might have been because of my martial arts background. I studied under three different senseis because I loved martial arts. I attended Nasir Ryu Ninjitsu in Manhattan on Mondays, Wednesdays, and Fridays, and Vee Arnis Jitsu on Tuesdays and Thursdays. On Saturdays or Sundays, whenever he was free, I studied Japanese-style jujitsu under Shareef Shabazz, who worked as a security guard on Nostrand and Fulton in Brooklyn for Arab clothing store owners.

Shareef was a Vietnam veteran. Because of his height, he was called a tunnel rat—a soldier who carried only a revolver and a knife to crawl through Vietcong tunnels, clear them, and plant explosives. It was an extremely dangerous job. He still carried a revolver tucked under his Nation of Islam pinstriped suit.

When he returned from the war, he faced discrimination and spitting from people, compounded by the horrors he had experienced and his anger at being drafted to kill other poor brown people. He joined the Nation of Islam's elite security force called the Fruit of Islam and became a black Muslim under the teachings of Elijah Muhammad. I learned a lot about life from him. Although he faced tremendous hardships during the war, his experiences made him a man everyone admired and feared. Even the police didn't mess with him; he was a legend. He was one of the reasons I eventually joined the Marines.

Now, let's return to me getting the shit kicked out of me, as that's what eventually motivated me to join the Marines. My martial arts skills helped me fend off the attackers long enough to escape. I made it home, bloody and bruised, and lay on the couch in the dark.

My mother entered the living room and switched on the lights. She didn't need to say a word; the look of disgust on her face spoke volumes. After a moment, she turned off the lights and went back to bed. I lay back on the couch in the darkness, staring up at the ceiling, knowing I had let her down. It was clear to me that I needed to change.

The Glimmer of Something Better

Not long after my near beating, I was watching television when an advertisement caught my attention. I was captivated as I watched it unfold. They promised to help you travel the world and pay for college—something I desperately needed—and they had guns. I liked guns; it was a legacy from watching old Rambo movies with my grandfather, John Burke (may he rest in peace). The ad was for the military—perhaps the Army or Navy; I can't quite recall—but I remember what happened next.

I rushed to my mother, exclaiming, "Mom, Mom, I just saw an ad about how they will help me pay for college and let me travel the world!" (I conveniently left out the part about the guns).

"Oh, you saw a military ad," she said.

"Yes," I replied, then asked, "So there's more than one branch?" My naivete led me to this realization. The next words are forever etched in my memory. "Mom, which one is the toughest?"

Her answer set me on my path. "Well, son, everyone loves the Marines."

The very next day, I found myself at the Marine Corps recruiter's office in downtown Brooklyn, peering through the window. I had a red rag in my back right pocket, Tim boots on with one pant leg rolled up, my hat on backward, a marijuana nose ring like Tupac Shakur's, gold caps on my teeth, and Cross Colours Farmer Brown overalls.

"May I help you?" the young recruiter asked.

"I'm here to learn how to bust guns!" I declared. He looked

bewildered and confused, unsure of how to respond, then smiled and said, "Well, come on in. You came to the right place."

The night before I was set to ship off to boot camp, I saw the Puerto Rican kid from my earlier encounter. I was on the J train heading home when he hopped into my train car. He saw me, but it was too late for him to get off; the doors closed behind him. A guy was sleeping at the end of the car, and the Puerto Rican kid was by the door to my left when I first noticed him. I stood up, twirling a razor blade I had learned to use from some members of my CRIME KING crew who'd done time. I also carried a box cutter in my pocket from my job at Love Stores, a once-famous NYC chain that sold health items similar to Walgreens or Rite-Aid.

Not wanting to look weak, he walked slowly to the opposite side of the pole dividing the train car to pass by me. He didn't make eye contact, despite clearly seeing that I was ready to engage. As he walked by, the tension grew. I gripped my box cutter tightly, sliding the blade out to prepare for any confrontation. I also concealed the razor blade in my left hand.

I glared at him as he slowly passed, but he avoided engaging with me. I took that as a sign that he didn't want to continue the conflict. He was probably carrying a gun, so things wouldn't have gone smoothly for me either if things escalated. As he walked away, I realized he was about my age. Had we lived on the same block, we might have been friends. Tomorrow, I was set to leave the hellhole that was Crimeville for the Marines, while he remained trapped there. It was a poetic tragedy that I didn't fully comprehend until I returned from military boot camp.

A Changed Man Returns

Three months later, I returned from Marine Corps boot camp in Parris Island, South Carolina. The plan was to stay with my mother in Brownsville, Brooklyn, for two weeks before heading off to my MOS school at Camp Geiger, North Carolina.

When my friend Ryan came around, he was surprised by how different I looked and acted. After greeting me, his expression turned serious.

"D's is looking for you," he said.

That startled me. "D's" referred to detectives, but I hadn't done anything illegal.

"Why?" I asked.

Ryan continued, "Remember that guy who jumped you in the club?"

"Yeah," I nodded. "The Puerto Rican kid and his crew."

"Yeah, that dude."

"What about him?" I inquired.

"D's wants to question you. You disappeared for three months, and while you were gone, someone shot him with a Mac 10 eleven times in front of his building!"

My heart sank—not because I felt any affection for the kid; I didn't really know him. The stark truth was that he was no different from me. We had simply chosen different paths. We all make choices in life and have paths laid out before us. The problem is that we often don't recognize we are at a crossroads until it's too late. I was in boot camp when this happened, but I still think about that moment on the train when he seemed like someone I could have been friends with. What might have changed if I had just said, "Hey bro, I'm leaving for boot camp. Why don't you join me?"

I remember him going his separate way in that train car without a word between us. I was not his enemy, nor was he mine. He was just a young guy like me, caught in the misfortune of growing up poor in the ghetto. I was fortunate to discover that the military was an option, and I took it. That young man lost his life at the hands of another lost soul, who may also be dead or in jail now.

If you take nothing else from this story, remember this: sometimes a path is laid out before you. Recognize your options and choose your direction wisely.

Escaping Hell

I recall telling my crew that I was joining the Marines. They questioned my decision. Sneaky wanted to know why I was going to fight a white man's war when there was a war right here on the streets.

I thought to myself, "Our parents rent. We don't own anything on these streets, not even the houses we live in."

I haven't seen those guys since I left Crimeville for my MOS school at Camp Geiger, North Carolina, all that time ago. I wish them well, but I suspect most are dead or in jail. None of those guys chose to be bad; it just happened because of their environment. The best thing a parent can do for their child is to move to a better environment at all costs.

A Breakdown of Brownsville, Brooklyn: Demographics of Hell

I'd like to provide some perspective on the area where I lived, worked, and suffered.

Brownsville, Brooklyn, the birth place of the Notorious Murder Inc. crime syndicate who operated from 1929 to 1941 and are responsible for over 400 murders. It's also the birthplace of Mike Tyson, Alfred Charles Sharpton Jr aka Rev. Al Sharpton, Larry King, and hardcore rappers like Smooth Da Hustler & his brother Trigga Tha Gambler and rap group M.O.P. Brownsville earned a notorious reputation as one of the most dangerous neighborhoods in America. During the late 1980s and early 1990s. The peak of violence and crime coinciding with the crack cocaine epidemic and gang violence held Brownsville as the official "murder capital of America" in any given year, it was widely recognized as one of the most violent areas in New York City and the nation during this period. Even as late as 2024 it is still considered the most dangerous neighborhood in NYC with a rate of crime of 1264 per 100,000 residence.

Key Points:

- **Late 1980s to Early 1990s:** During this period, Brownsville experienced alarmingly high rates of violent crime, including murders. I moved there in 1993 at 17 years old.
- **Contributing Factors:** The high crime rates were fueled by the crack epidemic, gang activity, economic decline, and ineffective law enforcement strategies.
- **Reputation:** Brownsville gained a notorious reputation as a dangerous area, widely acknowledged in media and public discussions during these years.

By the mid-1990s and into the 2000s, concerted efforts by law enforcement, community organizations, and shifts in social and economic conditions began to lower crime rates in Brownsville, although challenges still remain.

Brownsville is a residential neighborhood located in eastern Brooklyn, New York City. That hood shaped my outlook on life. I was born in Barbados, but came of age in Brownsville!

The Beginning of My Real Estate Journey

In October 2000, fresh off my last deployment in the Mediterranean and preparing for my transition out of the U.S. Marine Corps, I found myself researching my next steps in the library at Camp Lejeune, North Carolina.

On a whim, I typed "how to become a millionaire" into the search engine. An article titled "9 Out of Every 10 Millionaires in America Made Their Wealth in Real Estate" caught my attention. While music was my original passion, this piqued my interest in real estate and sparked thoughts about wealth in general.

THE TRUTH ABOUT WEALTH IN AMERICA

As I pondered the article, it increasingly resonated with me. I had lived in real estate my entire life; my family and friends did too. I'd been a tenant in apartment complexes and brownstones for as long as I could remember.

However, I had never considered that my landlord—the man who arrived in a beat-up old van, wearing dirty clothes and sporting greasy, soot-stained hands—might actually be a millionaire.

My perception of a millionaire had been distorted. I imagined someone like a rapper, posing next to a rented drop-top Corvette, adorned with fake gold chains and flashy rings, against the backdrop of a lavish mansion rented for a music video.

Here's a quick note: most millionaires don't fit that stereotype. They understand that maintaining wealth requires frugality and living under the radar. Flashy displays of wealth, like those seen with some rappers, often indicate one of two things: either the money isn't truly theirs, or they are spending it so rapidly that they risk running out.

Consider this: there are 22 million millionaires in the U.S. To put this in perspective, that's more people than live in the entire state of Florida, one of the most densely populated states in the nation, second only to California.

In fact, 8.8% of the U.S. population are millionaires. That's a substantial number of people with considerable wealth. It's likely that you know someone who knows a millionaire, and chances are that most individuals outside that millionaire's immediate family are unaware of their wealth.

What Does the Average Millionaire's Lifestyle Look Like?
Here's a snapshot:

- They focus on long-term success rather than short-term pleasures. They maintain a big-picture perspective and implement strategies to achieve their financial goals, understanding that frivolous spending can derail their dreams.
- They recognize the value of the right assets and invest in real estate along with other important options, such as stocks and bonds, to secure their earning potential.

A Note on the Gatekeepers

While many millionaires may not fit the typical image, they share certain traits. Some act as gatekeepers, believing that there should be barriers preventing others from accessing the opportunities they've worked hard to achieve. They want to erect tall walls between themselves and those they perceive as lesser.

I've always felt this way, but one experience really drove it home for me. I spoke with a man who had illegally immigrated to America and had built a successful life for himself and his family despite speaking very little English. He held an official state driver's license, financed a truck through a bank, and lived in a nice apartment.

However, he complained about the influx of new immigrants, believing they should all be sent back to their countries of origin. Ironically, he was still an illegal immigrant himself. He viewed the newcomers as threats to what he had, despite the fact that there was little difference between them and him.

Most people who discover the path to wealth tend to share this mindset. Once they find the secret, they often want to close the gates or build walls to keep others from gaining that knowledge. They fear that sharing their insights will somehow diminish their own success.

Many of my fellow real estate investors operate similarly. They'll offer some guidance, but it's often up to you to dig deeper and uncover the real secrets. Like those immigrants seeking a better life, you might have to hit rock bottom before you're willing to uproot your life in pursuit of something better.

I've been there, and I believe that these gatekeepers should instead be opportunity door openers. They should provide guidance and insights to those who are passionate and determined enough to pursue the American dream. This book aims to share hard-won insights from my journey as a successful real estate investor, distilled to provide you with what I never had: a helping hand to navigate this confusing and often frustrating world.

My own journey didn't start as auspiciously as I would have liked, and my entry into the industry came with a steep learning curve.

A LEARNING CURVE

Despite my initial passion for music, I found myself facing the disappointment that so many have experienced before me. After earning my music engineering certificate from the Institute of Audio Research in NYC (a regrettable use of my GI Bill), I quickly realized that fetching coffee for arrogant studio executives as an undervalued intern wouldn't make me rich. Frustrated, I turned my attention to real estate.

The beauty of real estate lies in its vast and varied nature. You don't have to start as an investor. I began my journey as a loan officer specializing in FHA mortgages before quickly obtaining my real estate license to generate more leads. All of this was happening while I worked as a security guard in Carteret, NJ, earning just $5 an hour. That experience taught me a valuable lesson: I never wanted to work for an hourly paycheck again.

The first mortgage I secured was for my own home—a quadplex (also known as a 4-family, 4-unit, or 4-plex) property in Newark, NJ. My brother Sebastian and I pooled our incomes to buy it, convincing the seller to contribute about $3,000 towards closing costs, which meant we only needed to put down 3%. We purchased the property for $147,000.

Our mortgage, including taxes and insurance, was approximately $1,300 a month, while our rental income from the other three units totaled around $1,600. After accounting for utilities like water, heat (which we paid), and common area lighting—approximately $200 a month—we cleared about $100 each month. Additionally, we saved the $600 we used to pay our previous landlord in North Newark.

In total, we either earned or saved about $700 each month. With that one real estate transaction, my brother and I transitioned from owning nothing but liabilities to owning an asset that generated cash flow. Our asset value jumped from $0 to $150,000 overnight, and we didn't even realize it!

CHAPTER 4

MY INTRODUCTION TO FLIPPING HOUSES

In 2002, I was a Realtor with a Realty Executives branch in Kearny, New Jersey, when my broker called me into his office. He had a real estate listing in Irvington, NJ, but preferred not to handle it himself. Instead, he asked if I could manage the listing for a friend of his. Eager for the opportunity, especially since I had mostly worked with buyers as a new agent, I gladly accepted.

Upon arriving at the property, I was horrified to find the door wide open, revealing a house filled with trash and clutter. It was so chaotic that I didn't even step inside. From the threshold, I could see the remnants of what was once a kitchen: cabinets torn off, copper pipes ripped from the walls, and what appeared to be human feces scattered across the floor.

I called my broker, Ken, to explain the situation, but he didn't seem surprised. After I described the wrecked house and its terrible condition, he simply suggested I see what we could get for it. At that moment, I decided to list it for $75,000, back in 2002, when house flipping was still a relatively unknown concept—long before reality TV shows like *Flip This House* educated the public on the business of property flipping.

For a long time, no one showed interest in the property. A few months later, I received a call from a man named Glen. Curious about his interest in such a rundown house, I asked what his plans were. He casually replied, "I'm going to buy it for $75,000, put in $25,000 worth of work, and sell it for about $150,000." Startled by his response, I asked if he intended to live there. He said no; it was strictly for investment purposes.

Up until that point, I had never considered a single-family home as an investment. Every buyer I had worked with wanted a place to live, not a profit. I did the math in my head: he was indicating he could net around $50,000 on this dilapidated property in a struggling neighborhood. He confirmed, "Yes."

Meanwhile, my commission, if another agent sold the property, would be 6% of $75,000, amounting to $1,125. Here was a random guy—who hadn't sourced the deal and didn't even know it existed until I listed it on the MLS—showing me that he could make $50,000 on a deal I controlled, while I would earn only between $1,125 and $2,250 (if I represented both sides of the sale). I was intrigued. Eager to learn, I asked Glen if he would teach me the business. While we didn't collaborate on my next two flips, we eventually worked together on three deals a few years later.

The dilapidated house in Irvington marked a turning point in my real estate career—a catalyst that ignited my desire to become a real estate investor. Glen opened my eyes to the vast disparity between the commissions I earned as a Realtor and the profits that could be realized through investing. This realization propelled me toward a path of wealth creation and financial independence.

Eager to uncover the secrets of real estate investing, I immersed myself in a journey of self-education. I devoured books, attended seminars, and sought guidance from seasoned investors who had successfully navigated this challenging landscape. Armed with knowledge and fueled by ambition, I was determined to carve my path to success.

However, before diving headfirst into investing, I encountered a valuable lesson that would shape my future partnerships and strengthen my resolve. In my pursuit of expanding my ventures, I entered into a partnership with someone whose intentions were far from noble—a painful realization that not all partnerships are built on trust and shared goals.

Raggedy Partnerships, Rich Lessons

Your mindset plays a significant role in the success you achieve (or fail to achieve). However, success isn't solely about individual effort; collaboration with others is essential.

We've discussed various partners, including contractors, subcontractors, skilled professionals, real estate agents, and more. If you genuinely want to achieve measurable success within a realistic timeframe and are not already financially well-off, forging partnerships is crucial.

The Challenge of Partnerships

The challenge? Partnerships can be difficult. It's often hard to distinguish between those who will help you succeed and those who might lead you astray. Sometimes, what appears to be a surefire opportunity can quickly turn into a disaster. Here's a personal story about my early partnerships, the mistakes I made, and the valuable lessons I learned.

Fledgling Partnerships and the Lessons Learned

I began my career as a loan officer, specializing in FHA mortgages for first-time homebuyers. My mentor, Ben (not his real name), was a flamboyant Italian mortgage broker with a commanding presence. He drove a shiny silver sports car, flaunted a diamond-studded gold chain that glimmered in the sunlight, and often recounted past encounters with local mafiosos. Despite his loud and brash style, I respected Ben for his financial expertise and enthusiasm, absorbing every piece of advice he offered.

My interest in real estate investing was sparked by a conversation with my friend Glen. Encouraged by Ben, I began to seriously consider this career path. Soon, Ben introduced me to Paul, another loan officer and successful investor. Paul advised us to connect with an REO (real estate owned) broker to explore opportunities in bank-owned properties.

I reached out to my realtor friend Manny, who was an experienced REO agent. Although he had no active listings, he knew of an investor trying to flip a property without making repairs. The investor had purchased a small single-family home in Irvington, NJ, for about $25,000 and hoped to sell it for $60,000. After some negotiation, we agreed on a purchase price of $45,000 and put the property under contract.

FINANCING WOES

However, we soon faced financing challenges. Traditional loans were not an option for a property in such poor condition, so we needed a hard money loan. Gala Resources in New York seemed like a good choice, but they refused to lend to inexperienced investors like us. Ben suggested that Paul join the partnership to co-sign the loan and lend his expertise. Paul agreed, and Ben, who would also co-sign, provided the 20% down payment. I would manage the renovations and handle the sale, with profits split three ways. Everything was set, and we sealed the partnership with a handshake—no formal agreement, just trust.

Next, we had to find contractors to bring our project to life. The first contractor's estimate was $50,000—far beyond our budget. The second estimate, from a local handyman, came in at just $10,000, but something didn't feel right, so we passed on his offer.

Eventually, we hired Denis, who agreed to complete the work for $25,000 because he was desperate for the job. He started on the exterior, but within two weeks, we had already spent $10,000 on roofing, windows, and siding. The following phases—plumbing, wiring, and interior renovations—cost another $15,000. With $25,000 already spent and the project incomplete, Denis ran out of funds and couldn't continue without additional financing.

After tense discussions, Ben and Paul agreed to cover the extra costs. I also contributed by doing some of the labor myself, utilizing sweat equity and my Home Depot credit card to keep things moving. We brought in another contractor, Ali, to finish the job, but further complications arose. At one point, the hot and cold water lines were crossed, and we discovered that the previous homeowners had poured cement down the sewer lines out of spite during foreclosure. These surprises forced us to exceed our budget by another $10,000.

SPLITTING THE PROFITS

Despite all the setbacks, we finally completed the renovations and found a buyer—a lovely Haitian woman thrilled to purchase the home. We sold the property for $140,000, marking a successful first deal. Even with the cost overruns, we were proud of what we had achieved as novice investors.

Encouraged by our success, we immediately dove into our next project, purchasing another single-family home in Irvington for $45,000 and investing an additional $35,000 in repairs. Including points, closing costs, and commissions, we had invested about $95,000 in the project and expected to see a $45,000 profit, which we planned to split equally—$15,000 each. But that's when things began to unravel.

An Eye-Opener and a Costly Object Lesson

When it was time to divide the profits, Ben, who had been managing the finances, claimed we hadn't made any profit at all. Despite my close involvement in the project and my meticulous tracking of expenses, Ben controlled the financial records and began withholding critical information. Paul and I soon realized that Ben had diverted the profits into his own pocket—around $60,000 in total—leaving us empty-handed.

Our partnership, built on trust and a handshake, had failed spectacularly. Ben, with his wise-guy persona, had exploited our naivety. Although we could have pursued legal action, I chose to cut my losses and move on. I wanted to leave Ben and this bitter experience behind.

Lessons Learned

This betrayal taught me several valuable lessons about partnerships:

1. **Get it in Writing**: Always document agreements, whether negotiating a purchase price or entering into a partnership. If it's not in writing, it can be changed —and often not in your favor.
2. **Clarify All Terms Upfront**: Clearly list all terms and expectations in the agreement. Never assume something is "understood."

3. **Sign and Notarize the Agreement**: A signature formalizes a deal into a binding contract. If someone hesitates to sign, walk away—they're likely not being honest.
4. **Trust, but Verify**: No matter how close your relationship, always verify that everything is clear, agreed upon, and documented.

Despite this painful experience, I remained resilient. I regrouped, armed with new insights about the importance of formalizing partnerships in writing, and continued my journey as a real estate investor. Through careful planning, clear communication, and legally binding agreements, I was able to protect my interests and build lasting, successful partnerships.

How We Transform R.A.G.S (Remedy Assets Give Solutions) into R.I.C.H.s (Readily Inhabitable Conforming Habitats)

At ReVelopers: The House Sellers 911, we specialize in converting R.A.G.S into R.I.C.H.s, which is the inspiration behind our book, *Raggedy Riches*. Real estate investment is not just a route to wealth for investors; it serves as a beacon of hope for those in financial distress, particularly the sellers we assist in avoiding ruin.

Imagine breathing new life into forgotten spaces and revitalizing cities, neighborhoods, and towns through strategic property rehabilitation. Here's a glimpse into this transformative process:

R.A.G.S (Remedy Assets Give Solutions)

- **Remedy Distressed Assets**: We excel at identifying

assets in need of rehabilitation and tailoring solutions
for their restoration and revitalization.

- **Awaken Potential**: We see the hidden possibilities
  within neglected properties, envisioning them as
  catalysts for positive change and community
  rejuvenation.
- **Give Back to the Community**: Committed to
  community engagement, we collaborate with local
  stakeholders to support the neighborhoods we serve.
- **Craft Creative Solutions**: We address unique
  property challenges with innovative approaches,
  maximizing their potential for positive impact and
  sustainable growth.

R.I.C.H (Readily Inhabitable Conforming Habitats)

- **Identify Opportunities**: We actively seek out
  neglected properties that can be revitalized and
  transformed into vibrant community hubs.
- **Inhabitable Rehabilitation**: Our focus is on ensuring
  that rehabilitated properties become livable and
  conducive to community well-being.
- **Conform to Standards**: We adhere to local
  regulations and community standards, promoting
  sustainable development and harmonious growth.
- **Harmonize with Habitats**: Beyond just buildings,
  we aim to create thriving environments that enhance
  community connectivity and well-being.

With R.A.G.S leading the way, every distressed asset
becomes an opportunity for renewal and regeneration. Together,
we embark on a journey to transform communities and build a
brighter future for all.

In the years that followed, I refined my skills as a renovator, developer, and landlord. I learned the intricacies of property management, the art of negotiation, and the importance of building strong relationships with contractors, lenders, and tenants. Each venture brought valuable lessons, and with every success and setback, my knowledge and expertise grew.

While partnerships remained a key aspect of my journey, I approached them with caution and discernment. I sought individuals who shared my vision, complemented my strengths, and brought unique perspectives to the table.

Trust was no longer given blindly; it was earned through transparency, accountability, and a proven track record of integrity.

Through trials and triumphs, I gradually built a portfolio of properties that became the foundation of my wealth. From humble single-family homes to expansive apartment complexes, each acquisition represented a step closer to financial independence. The profits I earned as an investor dwarfed the modest commissions I once received as a realtor, confirming the wisdom of my chosen path.

In the years to come, I would cross paths again with the investor, G, who had ignited my passion for real estate. This time, we would embark on ventures together, equipped with the lessons learned and a shared commitment to mutual success. Our partnership would flourish, solidified by trust and a mutual understanding of the risks and rewards. To truly thrive, however, we had to learn and master the four F's of property flipping, which we will discuss in the next chapter.

CHAPTER 5

THE RAGGEDY TO RICH PROCESS: THE FOUR F'S OF SUCCESSFUL HOUSE FLIPPING — FIND IT, FUND IT, FIX IT, AND FLIP IT

I n this chapter, we will explore the fundamental principles that drive successful house-flipping ventures: the Four F's: Find It, Fund It, Fix It, and Flip It. Mastering these four crucial steps will lay the foundation for your journey toward profitable real estate investments.

FIND IT: THE ART OF PROPERTY ACQUISITION

The first step is to identify a property with investment potential, which typically means purchasing it below market value. The best opportunities often arise from motivated sellers. Here are the types of properties I typically pursue:

1. **Foreclosures**
2. **Inherited Houses**
3. **Vacant Properties**
4. **Dilapidated Houses**
5. **Burnt-Out Landlords**

When we refer to "looking for a deal," we mean seeking

properties priced below market value. Investing in market-value properties will not yield the substantial gains you need, nor will it allow you to assist struggling owners in escaping their burdensome homes.

To kick off your house-flipping journey, you must find the right property. This process involves diligent research, market analysis, and a keen eye for opportunity. Consider the following strategies:

Market Research and Analysis

Conduct thorough market research to identify emerging neighborhoods, areas with growth potential, and properties that present favorable market conditions. Stay informed about local real estate trends, property values, and demographic changes.

To effectively conduct this research, here are some recommended tools:

- **Online Platforms:** Numerous online real estate platforms, like Zillow and Realtor.com, can serve as valuable starting points. However, remember that these platforms primarily exist to gather information from potential buyers and sell it to lenders and others in the industry, similar to social media sites. Use them for initial insights, but don't rely solely on them.
- **Multiple Listing Service (MLS):** The MLS is a privately owned database created by real estate professionals to facilitate home sales. Accessing your area's MLS requires membership in the National Association of Realtors (NAR), so building strategic alliances with realtors or brokers is crucial. The MLS offers more comprehensive and accurate information than other resources.

- **Census Information:** Every decade, the U.S. government conducts a census, which provides valuable data beyond just population counts. Census information can help you understand demographic shifts and the makeup of local communities. While much of the data is not publicly available, you can access relevant information at data.census.gov. This data will help you make informed decisions about house flipping.

Investing in existing neighborhoods—especially those facing economic downturns—can yield affordable properties. By renovating these homes, you can contribute to revitalizing entire areas, which can be even more rewarding than the financial gain from a simple home flip.

However, don't overlook newer neighborhoods. In certain regions, people may stay in a home for only three to five years and might need to move quickly. This trend is particularly prevalent near military bases and in technology corridors. Both methods of investment can complement each other; for instance, profits from a suburban flip can fund a more ambitious project aimed at rejuvenating an aging neighborhood.

Networking and Relationships

Cultivating a strong network within the real estate industry is essential. Attend events, join investment clubs, and build relationships with agents, brokers, and fellow investors. These connections can provide valuable insights and access to off-market deals.

Here's how to build your network effectively:

- **Real Estate Investment Clubs:** These clubs connect you with like-minded individuals, facilitating networking and potential deals. They can help you discover projects that may otherwise go unnoticed and enable you to participate in larger deals than you could manage alone. Remember, it's all about who you know and who they know; you're just a few connections away from significant opportunities.

- **Real Estate Agents:** Not all real estate agents will want to work with investors, and that's okay. Some agents prefer to deal exclusively with buyers and sellers. However, partnering with an investor-friendly agent can provide crucial benefits, including MLS access, identifying potential flip homes, monitoring your return on investment (ROI), and connecting you with other professionals, such as contractors and interior designers.
- **Real Estate Brokers:** Brokers manage their own real estate businesses and often oversee agents. Connecting with a broker can expand your reach to potential properties and introduce you to agents willing to work with investors.
- **Contractors:** It's vital to have a few trusted contractors on your list as you embark on your house-flipping journey. While you might handle some renovation work yourself, it's often more efficient to focus on other aspects of the flip or seek new investment opportunities. Look for a reliable general contractor who has connections with subcontractors, and consider hiring specialists such as HVAC professionals, electricians, plumbers, and carpenters.

Online Listings and Platforms

Utilize online resources like real estate websites, listing platforms, and online auctions to identify potential investment properties. Regularly scour these platforms for opportunities, using advanced search filters to narrow down your options.

I've already mentioned several real estate platforms, but let's take a more detailed look at the various options available and what each offers.

SMARTAPP

SMARTAPP is a groundbreaking, free-to-download application designed for the future of social commerce, particularly in real estate. It seamlessly integrates the buying and selling of homes, apartments, and other properties with a suite of social features. Users can share audio, videos, and photos, connect with others in real life, and forge meaningful relationships. Available on both iOS and Android, SMARTAPP was developed by my team and me to bridge the gap between buyers, investors, and real estate agents through social connections.

Since its inception, the app has evolved beyond simply providing real-time property listings across all 50 states. It now offers additional features such as generating Land Trust documents, checking the current weather, receiving daily horoscopes, managing digital business cards, and posting both informative and entertaining content. A standout feature is the social audio function, which allows for group chats similar to those on the Clubhouse audio app, but without the negative aspects that often lead to drama.

I encourage you to download SMARTAPP and follow me—it's also the best way to get in touch with me. We plan to introduce Direct Messaging (DMs) soon, and in the future, we will incorporate artificial intelligence to enhance efficiency for buyers, investors, and agents alike. If you're searching in the app stores, look for the "S" inside a gear logo.

. . .

Zillow

Zillow is free to use and offers a mobile app, boasting millions of users. Among real estate listing platforms (excluding MLS), it has the largest number of properties, with over 135 million listings. Zillow provides a "Zestimate," which is an estimate of a property's value created by the company's proprietary algorithm. However, this estimate can vary significantly due to inconsistencies in listing information, so take it with a grain of salt.

Realtor.com

Following Zillow is Realtor.com, which has nearly as many properties but offers something Zillow does not: 99% of MLS-listed properties can also be found here. It includes a mobile app as well. However, Realtor.com does not feature for-sale-by-owner (FSBO) listings, meaning home sellers cannot list their properties independently. Consequently, every property here incurs an additional cost in the form of the realtor's commission.

Trulia

With over a million properties listed, Trulia is a strong contender. It's free for users (but not for realtors or lenders) and has a mobile app. Trulia offers greater transparency than many other platforms, along with plenty of local information and built-in real estate guides. However, FSBO properties are not permitted.

Foreclosure.com

For home flippers, Foreclosure.com is a valuable resource, as banks aim to sell foreclosed properties rather than retain ownership. This platform connects you with distressed properties that you can buy, renovate, and flip. However, access to the site requires a subscription, costing approximately $40 per month, plus another $40 per month for the mobile app.

FSBO.com

FSBO.com caters specifically to homeowners who wish to list their properties themselves. However, you'll find fewer listings compared to other platforms, and there is no mobile app available.

Fund It: Navigating the World of Financing

Once you've identified a promising property, the next step is securing the necessary funding for acquisition. While traditional financing options may be available, exploring alternative sources can provide greater flexibility and expedite the process. From my experience, every flip is unique, so I highly recommend being adaptable in your financing methods.

I've worked with traditional lenders as well as individuals and real estate investment groups. However, conventional lenders are often reluctant to finance house flips, as these ventures fall outside their typical risk profiles. Their business model is focused on minimal risk and predictable returns, whereas house flipping inherently involves greater risk. So, what are your options?

Private Lenders vs. Hard Money Lenders

Understanding the differences between private lenders and hard money lenders is crucial for financing house flipping projects, as each offers distinct advantages and terms that can significantly impact your investment journey.

1. Definition and Structure

Private Lenders

•Individuals or small groups of investors who provide funds for real estate projects.

•Typically operate independently or as informal lending groups.

•Often have personal relationships with borrowers, leading to a more customized lending experience.

Hard Money Lenders

•Usually institutions, companies, or private equity firms that lend against the property itself.

•Operate similarly to traditional banks but focus specifically on real estate investments.

•Have a more structured process due to their larger operational frameworks.

2. Application Process

Private Lenders

•Generally have a more relaxed application process.

•Often do not require formal applications, credit checks, or extensive documentation of assets.

•Focus primarily on the presented deal, assessing potential profitability and the borrower's experience.

Hard Money Lenders

•Require a formal loan application process.

•Typically perform credit checks and may request documentation of income and assets.

•Evaluate risk based on both the property's value and the borrower's financial background.

3. Funding Speed and Flexibility

Private Lenders

•Can fund deals quickly, sometimes on the same day if all necessary information is in order.

•Offer more flexible terms based on personal negotiations.

•May be willing to adjust terms to better suit your needs, depending on established relationships.

Hard Money Lenders

•While they also provide fast funding, the process usually takes longer than with private lenders due to required paperwork.

•Funding timelines typically range from a few days to a week.

•Offer less flexibility, as they adhere to corporate policies.

4. Loan Amounts and Down Payments

Private Lenders

•May provide up to 100% funding of project costs, depending on their risk assessment.

•Often base funding on a 65%-75% Combined Loan to Value (CLTV) metric, calculated from the After Renovation Value (ARV).

•Down payment requirements vary significantly, with some offering 100% funding for attractive deals.

Hard Money Lenders

•Typically require a down payment of 20% for purchases, necessitating some upfront equity from the borrower.

•Often finance 70%-80% of the ARV or the purchase price, whichever is lower.

•Borrowers must have cash on hand to cover the remaining 20%.

5. Interest Rates and Fees

Private Lenders

•Tend to offer lower interest rates compared to hard money lenders, as they may not be driven by profit maximization.

•Generally have lower fees, with some private lenders negotiating no fees if a trusting relationship exists.

•Terms may be more favorable depending on the private lender's investment goals.

Hard Money Lenders

•Typically charge higher interest rates, ranging from 8% to 15% or more, reflecting the associated risk and speed of funding.

•Often impose upfront fees, loan origination fees, and points (a percentage of the total loan amount).

•These costs can accumulate quickly, affecting your project's overall profitability.

6. Relationships and Communication

Private Lenders

•Foster personal relationships with borrowers, often communicating in a direct and informal manner.

•Strong relationships can lead to better terms, quicker funding, and a more supportive lending experience.

•They are often willing to collaborate on terms that benefit both parties.

Hard Money Lenders

•Relationships are typically more transactional and less personal, as they handle numerous clients and may have stricter borrower criteria.

•Communication tends to be more formal and may involve multiple layers of decision-makers.

•Hard money lenders often focus more on their bottom line than on the relationship itself.

7. Sourcing Lenders

Private Lenders

• **Networking**: Attend local real estate investment groups, networking events, or meetups. Personal connections can lead to funding opportunities.

• **Referrals**: Seek referrals from real estate agents, attorneys, or other professionals in the field who might know potential investors.

• **Online Platforms**: Utilize social media or dedicated online investment platforms where private investors seek opportunities.

• **Direct Approach**: Reach out directly to friends, family, or colleagues interested in real estate investing.

Hard Money Lenders

• **Research Online**: Many hard money lenders have websites detailing their services, terms, and loan programs. Use search engines to find reputable lenders in your area.

• **Real Estate Associations**: Explore local real estate associations or investment groups, which often provide lists of recommended hard money lenders.

• **Referrals**: Just like with private lenders, asking fellow investors or professionals can lead you to trustworthy hard money lenders.

• **Real Estate Brokers**: Some brokers have established relationships with hard money lenders and can refer clients to them.

Both private and hard money lenders play crucial roles in financing house flipping projects, but they serve different needs and come with different terms. Understanding these distinctions will help you choose the right financing for your specific situation.

• **Choose Private Lenders** if you seek flexible terms, lower costs, and quick access to funds without extensive paperwork. Their personalized approach can maximize your investment potential.

• **Opt for Hard Money Lenders** if you value speed and reliability in funding, while being prepared for higher costs and down payment requirements. Their structured process may suit borrowers looking for a quick cash solution, although it comes at a higher price.

By recognizing these differences and knowing how to source each type of lender, you can strategically select the best financing option to support your real estate investment ambitions.

Creative Financing

Don't assume your only funding options are hard money/private money loans or conventional lenders. There are numerous ways to access the funds you need for fixing and flipping. Explore creative financing options such as seller financing, partnerships, or joint ventures. These strategies can provide unique funding opportunities and shared risk. Here's a brief overview of each:

Seller Financing

Seller financing occurs when the seller agrees to finance the sale of the home directly to you, similar to a private money loan but without involving a private or hard money lender.

Before pursuing this option, ensure that the seller can finance the loan, meaning there is either no mortgage on the property or the existing mortgage does not contain a "due on sale" clause, which requires full repayment upon the sale and typically prohibits seller financing.

Once verified, discuss the specifics with the seller. Each seller financing agreement is unique, but it should address critical aspects such as interest rate, down payment, amortization period, balloon payment specifics, and your plans if you haven't paid off the loan or refinanced by the end of the term.

Be prepared to provide a cash down payment, and keep in mind that the interest rate may not be as favorable as what you would receive from a traditional lender if the seller cannot manage financial risk effectively.

Partnerships

Forming a partnership can be another viable funding option. These relationships can be mutually beneficial, allowing both you and your partner to build wealth through successive flips.

Partnerships can take various forms; one partner might provide funding while the other handles property scouting and renovations. Flexibility in partnership arrangements is key, as you might partner with a significant other, sibling, family member, friend, or even a business acquaintance.

However, don't let an existing relationship give you a false sense of security. All successful partnerships begin with due diligence. Ensure that potential partners are financially solvent and have no negative marks in their history. Transparency and trust are essential.

Additionally, it's wise to plan for worst-case scenarios. Being prepared is not only smart but also a good business practice.

Joint Ventures

While you may be more familiar with the term "joint ventures" in the context of investing in startups, they also play a significant role in the real estate industry. Think of joint ventures as opportunities to pool resources with others; it's like an amplified partnership.

A joint venture typically involves two or more entities, often businesses. While partnerships are the most basic form of joint ventures, there are numerous other configurations. In many cases, one or more entities provide funding for a property flip in exchange for a specified return on their investment upon successful completion. Other entities might contribute industry connections, equipment, expertise, or other valuable resources.

Most joint ventures will have one entity that supplies the majority of the funding and another that handles the bulk of the renovation work. However, the circle of collaborators can be expanded. Consider including general contractors, subcontractors, and other professionals who are essential for home flips. While this may result in a smaller share of the profits, partnering with others can lead to faster completion of flips, potentially outweighing the reduction in profit share.

Fix It: Turning Rags into Riches

With the property acquired and funding secured, it's time to unleash your creativity and renovate to maximize the property's value. Revel in the expertise of what some might call rehabbers, who excel in strategic renovations and cost-effective improvements. Consider the following best practices:

Create a Detailed Renovation Plan

Conduct a thorough property inspection to develop a comprehensive renovation plan. Prioritize repairs and upgrades based on market demands and potential returns on investment. Your renovation plan should be structured in stages, beginning with essential structural repairs and followed by aesthetic updates. Typically, this plan is developed in two stages: a rough work schedule created when financing is secured, followed by a more detailed plan once the property is acquired, especially if permits need to be submitted for approval.

For example, if you purchase a 30-year-old home that has

been neglected, you might find it needs a fresh coat of paint inside and out, minor siding replacements, and upgraded windows. However, upon closer inspection, you may discover that the roof and parts of the sub-roof require replacement.

In this scenario, you should prioritize replacing the roof and sub-roof before proceeding with any other renovations. While it's best to catch these issues during the initial inspection, even experienced inspectors can miss problems.

Your renovation plan should start with the roof replacement, followed by other priority repairs. Next, include elements that bring the property up to date, such as replacing aging carpeting with cost-effective options like wood-grain laminate (e.g., Pergo). Focus on high-return, moderate-to-low-cost improvements, including:

- Minor bathroom remodels
- Landscape upgrades
- Minor kitchen remodels
- Doors
- Siding
- Lighting

An accurate and up-to-date budget is the foundation of your renovation plan. This budget will guide everything about the flip, from the quality of flooring you can install to the extent of renovations in the kitchen and bathrooms. Additionally, it should include a holding budget, as most home flips require a period when the property is unoccupied, incurring costs.

Engage Reliable Contractors

Establish a network of trustworthy contractors, subcontractors, and tradespeople specializing in house renovations. Seek recommendations, review portfolios, and obtain multiple bids before selecting contractors for your projects.

You can approach this in a couple of ways. First, you might

choose to hire contractors independently. This is advisable if you plan to do some of the work yourself or if you have experience as a general contractor or inspector, allowing you to oversee the work being done. This approach gives you greater control over the project.

Alternatively, you can hire a general contractor, who will have an established network of contractors, subcontractors, and tradespeople necessary to complete the work. While this option saves you time and allows you to focus on finding additional properties to flip, it may reduce your control and typically comes at a higher cost than hiring contractors directly.

However, the expertise and existing connections of a general contractor can be invaluable. The time and stress saved by working with a general contractor often outweigh any increase in costs.

Regardless of whether you choose to hire a general contractor or manage contractors yourself, thorough vetting is essential. While price is an important factor, it should not be your primary consideration. Always obtain multiple bids for each project and compare itemized descriptions to understand what each includes. Lower prices may sometimes indicate fewer services, so ensure you ask for itemized bids.

When vetting contractors or general contractors, follow this checklist:

- Request proof of licensure.
- Request proof of insurance.
- Request itemized bids.
- Ask for references and follow up with them.
- Check the Better Business Bureau (https://www.bbb.org).
- Verify current licenses with your state's licensing authority.
- Ask questions to ensure clarity on project details.

Stick to a Budget and Schedule

Develop a detailed renovation budget and adhere strictly to it. Maintain open communication with contractors, track progress, and promptly address any issues to keep the project on schedule.

To create a detailed, accurate budget, follow the 65% rule in house flipping. (In some areas, particularly in competitive markets like New York and California, this figure may need to rise to 75% to remain competitive. However, for the majority of the real estate market, 65% is the norm.) Essentially, your total costs should not exceed 65% of the home's value after repairs, minus renovation costs. The after-repair value (ARV) is the estimated sale price of the home once all repairs and renovations are complete.

To determine if a home is worth your investment, follow these steps:

1. Estimate After-Renovation Value: Assess how much you believe the home will be worth after renovations. Utilize local comparable properties, MLS pricing, and other resources to arrive at the most accurate estimate possible.

2. Calculate Maximum Offer: Multiply your estimated after-renovation value by 65% to 75%, depending on the area, risk factors, your risk tolerance, and your lender's requirements.

3. Determine Your Budget: Subtract your estimated renovation costs from this new amount.

4. Evaluate the Result: Ensure that the resulting figure matches the purchase price you plan to pay for the property or is higher than that amount.

. . .

Estimating repair costs is a crucial part of your renovation budget. While there's no universal list of necessary renovations, here are some common upgrades for flip homes:

- Kitchen updates (counters, cabinets, sink, backsplash, island, etc.)
- Bathroom improvements (vanities, sinks, mirrors, lighting)
- New flooring throughout the home
- Interior and exterior painting
- Energy efficiency upgrades (new windows, etc.)
- HVAC system repairs or upgrades
- Replacement of exterior doors and hardware
- New interior lighting
- Landscaping, exterior pressure washing, fence repair or replacement, and other curb appeal enhancements

The key is to identify high-value, low to moderate-cost upgrades that appeal to potential buyers in the area. For instance, investing heavily in a gourmet kitchen with luxury features may not be wise in a predominantly blue-collar neighborhood.

Conducting a Home Inspection: Before purchasing, walk through the home and make a list of desired upgrades. Use this list to obtain price estimates from home improvement stores like Lowe's or Home Depot, which will help you refine your budget. The more information you gather beforehand, the easier it will be to stick to your budget.

Communication with Contractors: Effective communication with your contractors is vital. Without it, you risk misalignment, leading to cost overruns, missed deadlines, and wasted materials.

Here are some strategies I've developed throughout my flipping career to ensure effective communication:

1.Regular Site Visits: Make a point to visit the worksite regularly. Don't let your search for your next flip keep you away for too long; aim for at least once a week if you aren't doing hands-on work yourself. This allows you to observe progress, discuss concerns with contractors and crews, and catch potential issues early.

2.Set Clear Expectations: Contractors are busy, but they understand the importance of meeting client expectations. If you request weekly updates, they should be happy to comply. However, these updates do not replace the need for in-person visits; accountability is key to ensuring your contractors stay on track.

3.Share Contact Information: A common communication barrier is outdated or incorrect contact information. Ensure contractors have your phone number, email address, and any other necessary contact details (like your Facebook Messenger). Likewise, verify you have the correct information for your contractors.

FLIP IT: MAXIMIZING RETURNS AND SELLING STRATEGICALLY

The final step in the house flipping process is selling the renovated property and enjoying the fruits of your labor. A successful flip requires effective marketing, strategic pricing, and a solid exit strategy. Consider these tactics:

Professional Staging and Photography: Showcase the property at its best by using professional staging and photography. Create an inviting atmosphere that highlights the property's unique features and appeals to potential buyers.

What Is Staging? Home staging involves presenting a home so it appears "lived in" but enhanced with a designer's touch. It can be minimalist or maximalist, each with its pros and cons.

At its core, staging aims to help potential buyers envision themselves in the home. It's about forging a connection and evoking an emotional response. Since everyone has different tastes, avoid overly specific themes (like formal, Art Deco, or French country). Instead, blend various elements to create a cohesive look that enhances the home's best features.

Strategic Pricing: Set an optimal selling price based on thorough market analysis, comparable sales, and the property's condition. Strive to strike a balance between maximizing returns and attracting potential buyers. The goal is to identify a "sweet spot" that appeals to buyers while optimizing your return on investment (ROI).

Understanding Market Analyses

A market analysis provides essential information for developing a pricing strategy. While conducting this analysis requires some effort, the benefits are significant. I break down my process into six key steps:

1. **Historical Data:** Begin by examining historical data for the area. Analyze past performance trends, including fluctuations in pricing and sales volume over time. I recommend utilizing reports from the National Association of Realtors (NAR) for comprehensive insights.
2. **Get to Know the Neighborhood:** A home's appeal is often tied to its surrounding neighborhood. Investigate the area's amenities, such as shopping, dining, and nightlife. Assess the crime rate and consider factors like walkability, bikeability, and proximity to major employment centers.

3. **Cast a Wide Net:** I strongly advocate for using multiple information sources. Relying on a single source can lead to bias, as they are often created for specific purposes. Gather data from community websites, news outlets, real estate authorities, and other resources to form an accurate picture.

4. **Know the Local Market:** Your real estate flipping efforts will be influenced by two major factors: the national real estate market and the local market. Of the two, the local market has the greatest impact. Stay informed about local conditions—whether it's a buyer's or seller's market.

5. **Future Development:** Consider the future of the area. Will it remain predominantly residential? Are there plans for new businesses or industries to establish themselves nearby?

6. **Be Dispassionate:** It's easy to become emotionally attached to your flip and overestimate its value. Approach the analysis critically, relying on hard data and actionable information.

Delving into Comparable Sales

If you've watched fix-and-flip TV shows or are involved in real estate investments, you're likely familiar with the term "comps," short for "comparable properties." Understanding comps is crucial for your pricing strategy, but what qualifies as a comp?

For a property to be considered comparable, it must share key similarities with the home you're flipping. This includes being of similar age, having the same number of bedrooms and bathrooms, and a lot size that is at least somewhat comparable. Ideally, comps should fall within 10% to 20% of your home's square footage and share similar features (for example, a home with a pool cannot be compared to one without).

. . .

Here's a checklist of items to compare when identifying your comps:

- Number of bedrooms
- Number of bathrooms
- Square footage
- Lot size and shape
- Elevation
- Original construction date
- Level and date of any renovations
- Similar architectural design
- Number of stories or floors
- Special features (e.g., swimming pool, freestanding garage)
- Same neighborhood
- Same school zone
- Similar condition at the time of sale
- Previous sales data (price, date, etc.)

The Effect of Property Condition

The condition of your flip property significantly impacts your pricing strategy. For example, a 50-year-old home with minimal renovations will likely sell for a much lower price than a fully modernized home built 20 years ago, assuming all other factors are equal. Key considerations regarding property condition include:

- Condition of the kitchen
- Condition of the bathrooms
- Condition of the bedrooms
- Age of appliances (stovetop, oven, refrigerator, water heater, HVAC system, etc.)

- Condition of the roof
- Condition of the foundation
- Condition of the lot/yard
- Costs for necessary updates to meet compliance standards
- Costs for modernizations to remain competitive with similar properties

Bringing It All Together

After completing a thorough market analysis, examining nearby comps, and assessing the property's condition relative to the comps, you can formulate a pricing strategy. Your goal is to position the property as an attractive option for your target buyer.

So, who is your target buyer? There isn't a one-size-fits-all answer. For instance, a two-bedroom, two-bath house with 1,200 square feet might be ideal for first-time homebuyers or older couples looking to downsize. However, these two groups often have different needs regarding layout, space utilization, and appliance quality.

Consider your target audience carefully, then analyze pricing for similar properties in the area. Determine how to position your property to stand out while remaining competitive. This information will be critical not just for setting your price, but also for marketing and promotion.

Effective Marketing and Promotion

To effectively market your property, develop a comprehensive plan that highlights its key selling points. Utilize online listings, social media platforms, and traditional marketing channels to reach a broad audience of potential buyers.

Identifying Your Key Selling Points

In the previous section, we discussed setting your pricing strategy and comparing your property to others in terms of both price and features. These factors are essential for your marketing and promotional efforts. Focus on your home's unique selling points. Here are some key aspects to consider:

1. Design

The design of your home can be a significant selling point, especially if it stands out from cookie-cutter properties. Older homes from the 1950s, 60s, and 70s often feature unique characteristics, such as sunken living rooms and built-ins. Highlight any distinctive design elements or construction features that could attract potential buyers.

2. Space

The amount of space in your home is another important selling point. Consider how the square footage can appeal to different buyers, such as growing families or those needing to accommodate aging loved ones. However, keep in mind that larger homes are not always more sellable; factors like market demand and local trends (e.g., demographics of buyers) play a crucial role.

3. Location

The real estate mantra "location, location, location" remains paramount. Understanding how location impacts potential buyers is essential. Evaluate your home's proximity to various amenities and features, such as:

- Distance to employment centers
- Accessibility to main highways

- Proximity to major roadways and intersections
- Availability of shopping and dining options
- Nearby commercial or industrial developments
- Quality of the local school district, including choices among multiple districts
- Neighborhood maintenance, including mature trees and green spaces
- Nearby parks and recreational trails
- Access to state or national parks

By assessing these factors, you can tailor your marketing approach to appeal to different buyer segments.

4. Updates

While some buyers seek fixer-uppers, many prefer homes that require minimal repairs. If you've made updates, leverage these improvements to distinguish your property. Focus on high-impact updates that will draw attention in your marketing materials, such as:

- HVAC system upgrades (especially energy-efficient options)
- New flooring
- Modern lighting
- Attic conversions
- Finished basements
- New decks, patios, or porches
- Updated windows
- Sunrooms or bonus rooms

5. Curb Appeal

Don't overlook the importance of exterior appeal. A home

that looks uninviting from the street will deter potential buyers from exploring the interior. Enhancing curb appeal can be straightforward:

- Apply a fresh coat of exterior paint
- Invest in landscaping, including new plants, flowerbeds, shrubs, and trees
- Pressure wash the driveway
- Clean or replace aging gutters
- Ensure your home looks as good as or better than neighboring properties

6. Outbuildings

Today, many homeowners seek spaces adjacent to their homes that serve various purposes, from storage to hobbies. Outbuildings can be valuable assets in your marketing materials. If the property you're flipping includes any of the following, or if you can add them at a reasonable cost, be sure to feature them prominently in your marketing efforts:

- Storage buildings
- She-sheds
- Garden sheds
- Pool houses
- Detached garages
- Greenhouses
- Detached carports
- Gazebos
- Barns
- Tool sheds

7. Kitchen

The kitchen is the most frequently used room in nearly every home. It's where families gather for breakfast, children do homework, and late-night conversations over bowls of ice cream or glasses of wine take place. Therefore, the kitchen is the most crucial element to highlight in your marketing efforts.

If you have the budget, consider investing significantly in a modern kitchen renovation to showcase in your marketing materials. Here are the most impactful upgrades to prioritize:

- Kitchen island (new or updated)
- Cabinets (refreshed, painted, or replaced)
- Appliances (upgraded)
- Countertops (replaced)
- Lighting (task lighting, under-cabinet lighting, and overall illumination)
- Backsplash (extend as high as your budget allows for a striking effect)
- Flooring (replace outdated vinyl with new vinyl, tile, hardwood, or natural stone)

8. Baths

While the kitchen sees the most activity, bathrooms have evolved into serene spaces for relaxation and rejuvenation. This is especially true for the master bathroom, although updating secondary baths can also add value. Focus primarily on the master bath while considering enhancements for the others. Here are some key features to consider highlighting in your marketing:

- New stand-up shower
- New soaking tubs
- Updated lighting
- New flooring (tile or natural stone)
- New vanities
- New light fixtures

- Smart technology (smart mirrors, heated toilet seats, etc.)

9. Master Bedroom

The master bedroom has transformed into a sanctuary for rest and relaxation, not just a place to sleep and dress. When renovated and marketed effectively, it can feel like a spa or a tranquil retreat.

While updates may be limited by the existing layout, unless you have the budget for structural changes, some key updates include:

- Fresh paint (preferably in calming, restful tones)
- New window treatments (beyond traditional mini-blinds)
- New bedroom and closet doors
- Updated hardware (door handles, kick plates, etc.)
- Lighting in closets
- New bedroom lighting
- A designated sitting/dressing area

10. Backyard

Just as interior spaces have evolved, so have our expectations for outdoor areas. Today, homeowners desire outdoor spaces that reflect their lifestyles and allow for more time spent outside. Effective updates to the backyard can significantly enhance the property's marketability.

Consider the following popular updates that can elevate your marketing efforts, keeping in mind that factors such as property size, topography, and light exposure will influence your options:

- Outdoor kitchens
- Outdoor bars
- Gazebos and pergolas

- Patios, porches, and decks
- Pools and hot tubs (note that these can be divisive; some buyers prefer them, while others wish to avoid them)
- Expansive lawns for children and pets
- Fences
- Mature trees, including fruit and nut varieties

11. **Flexible Areas**

In the past, homes typically featured a few bedrooms, a kitchen, a dining room, a living room, and a couple of bathrooms. Today, homeowners seek more adaptable spaces that can cater to their changing needs. Flexible areas can be significant selling points, offering versatility and the potential for customization. Consider promoting the following flexible spaces in your marketing:

- Bonus rooms
- Game or family rooms
- Home theaters
- Converted attics
- Finished basements
- Home offices
- Entertainment rooms/home theaters
- Mud and laundry rooms

How to Maximize the Value of Online Listings

In the past, buying a home involved flipping through local real estate magazines, collaborating with a realtor, and visiting multiple properties in person. The Internet has revolutionized this process, allowing buyers to explore dozens of homes in a single day—all from the comfort of their couches.

While this transformation is liberating for both buyers and

sellers, it also means that your online listings must meet higher expectations. To attract the right buyers and encourage them to schedule a viewing or contact you, it's essential to maximize the impact of your listings. Here's a crash course on how to do that.

1. Utilize Multiple Listing Tools

Begin by identifying the listing websites you will use. If you're selling your home independently, platforms like Zillow and FSBO (For Sale By Owner) are invaluable. If you're working with a realtor, ensure your home is listed on Zillow, Realtor.com, and the MLS (Multiple Listing Service). Avoid relying on just one platform; potential buyers have different preferences. Some may favor Zillow, while others prefer Realtor.com or different sites. By using multiple listing tools, you can reach a broader audience.

2. Capture High-Quality Photos

High-quality photos are crucial for effective online listings. Include numerous images of both the home's exterior and interior. Ensure that your photos are clear and showcase each space in the best possible light—without being misleading. While a smartphone may suffice for most shots, consider investing in specialty lenses for better results or hiring a professional photographer to enhance the visual appeal of your home.

3. Craft an Engaging Property Description

While most buyers will first focus on your photos, many will later return to read the property's description. Therefore, it's vital to create a compelling description that highlights key details that buyers look for, such as:

- Square footage
- Number of bedrooms and bathrooms (including full and half baths)
- Year built
- Notable additions, updates, or upgrades
- Proximity to business and school districts
- Availability of high-speed Internet access, cable, etc.
- Sewer/septic information
- Municipal water/well status
- Key features, such as expansive outdoor decks, flexible bonus rooms, or completely upgraded kitchens

When writing your description, keep the following in mind:

- **Tell a Story:** Provide a comprehensive view of the home while helping potential buyers envision themselves living there. Aim for a blend of sales copy and prose.
- **Check for Errors:** Use correct spelling and punctuation. If buyers struggle to read your description or grasp the home's features, you may experience fewer showings and a longer time to sell.
- **Include a Call to Action:** Clearly instruct potential buyers on what to do next. Should they call or email you? Is the property open for walk-throughs? A strong call to action encourages buyers to take the next step.

4. Leverage Listing Service Features

Each listing service has unique layouts that can enhance your listing. For example, Zillow includes a "What's Special" section at the top of the property page, just below the details and images.

Use this space to highlight features that set your home apart, such as "built-in pantry," "gas fireplace," "new HVAC," "new roof," or "split floorplan."

5. Highlight the Neighborhood

Don't limit your description to just the home and its immediate surroundings. Provide information about the area, as location is a critical factor in many buyers' decisions. Mention nearby amenities, such as shopping, dining, parks, or proximity to major highways. This context can help buyers appreciate the advantages of your home's location.

6. Optimize for Search Engines

While many buyers will find your property through the listing platform, remember that your listings can also appear in Google and Bing searches. Consider using the following keywords to enhance visibility:

- "For sale"
- "Single-family home," "apartment," "townhome," etc.
- Specific locations, such as "Atlanta," "Washington, DC," or "New York City"

7. Break Up Your Description

To enhance readability, break your property description into small paragraphs that guide the reader's eye downward. A wall of text can deter potential buyers, even if the home meets their criteria.

Writing an effective property description is crucial when selling your flip home, but it's not the only step. Understanding the role of social media is equally important in today's market.

You may wonder, "Why should I use social media to sell my flip property? Isn't an online real estate platform sufficient?" While many people do use online platforms, social media sites like The SMART app, Facebook, and X can significantly expand your reach.

Why Use Social Media?

1. **Widespread Reach**: Social media provides access to a vast audience. Facebook alone has around 3 billion monthly users. When you consider other platforms like Instagram, Threads, X, and Snapchat, the potential audience grows exponentially.
2. **Cost-Effective**: Most social media platforms are free to use, allowing you to reach a broad audience without incurring costs. In contrast, many real estate-specific platforms charge sellers for listing and marketing tools, meaning you can retain more of your profits from the sale.
3. **Engaging Content**: You can maximize your visibility and engage potential buyers by combining text, photos, and videos. Crafting an eye-catching Facebook post that highlights your home's key features can create an interactive experience that appeals to today's audience.
4. **Paid Tools**: You can opt to use paid tools to enhance your property listings. However, if you're flipping your first home, I recommend focusing on mastering the free features before considering paid options like Facebook lead ads.

Which Platforms Should You Use?

There isn't a one-size-fits-all solution for social media, so it's wise to experiment with different platforms to find what works best for you. Here are a few must-have platforms to consider:

- **Smart App**: This app is one of the best social commerce platforms in the real estate industry. It allows you to search for properties and conduct real estate business in a social-commerce environment. Look for Smart Realty and download it using the gear logo.
- **Facebook**: Often regarded as the most important social media tool, Facebook offers extensive free resources and options to expand your reach through paid promotions. Don't overlook Facebook Marketplace, which is very popular.
- **YouTube**: Ideal for sharing videos and showcasing your property, YouTube allows you to create videos and share links on other social media platforms for broader exposure. Note that for Facebook, it's best to use its native video posting options to avoid post suppression.
- **TikTok**: Despite some controversy, TikTok is a powerful selling tool that can help you build your audience and highlight your flip homes. Leverage TikTok trends for an organic boost, and consider using its paid sales tools if desired.
- **Instagram**: This platform lets you combine photos, videos, and text to create compelling posts that capture the attention of potential buyers. It is especially popular among individuals aged 25 to 45, a key demographic for home buyers.

These four platforms are just the beginning. As you delve into social media, explore additional options. The SMART app and X can be excellent for linking back to your other accounts, while LinkedIn can help expand your network, even if it's not primarily for selling. Pinterest may also be worth exploring.

Must-Have Traditional Marketing Channels

While digital tools and platforms often steal the spotlight, it's essential not to overlook traditional marketing channels. Sometimes, going analog can be the most effective way to generate interest in your flip home. But what exactly qualifies as "traditional" marketing today? Here's a quick overview:

Signage: Nothing is more traditional than placing a large "For Sale" sign in your front yard. You can usually find one at your local big-box store for just a few dollars. Choose a brightly colored sign that's large enough for passersby to see easily.

If there's space on the sign, include your phone number or email address. Otherwise, print flyers or handouts with your contact information so potential buyers can easily reach you. In addition to placing a "For Sale" sign in the front yard, consider putting signs in visible side yards and at key intersections nearby to attract more attention.

Flyers: Flyers are a staple of traditional marketing. Keep some at your front door or in a waterproof container next to your yard sign. Distribute them on windshields in local shopping centers, hand them out at networking events, and post them on bulletin boards in local stores. Your flyers should include essential details, such as:

- A large photo of the home's exterior
- Your name
- Your preferred contact method (email or cell phone)
- The home's price

- The home's address
- A brief list of features (e.g., 2 bed/2 bath split floor plan with a massive backyard)

Publications: Every geographic area has local publications that can help you market your home. Consider using:

- Local and regional newspapers
- Community newsletters and "nickel" publications
- Local real estate publications

Open House: Open houses are a crucial element in flipping homes. They provide potential buyers (and their agents) an opportunity to tour the property. While you can host an open house for an unfurnished property, staging can significantly enhance its appeal. Just be sure to hold your open houses after all renovations are complete.

Congratulations! You've embarked on the exciting journey of house flipping, armed with the knowledge of the Four F's: Find It, Fund It, Fix It, and Flip It. By mastering each step and implementing best practices, you can navigate the challenges of property acquisition, secure financing, execute strategic renovations, and ultimately sell your transformed property for maximum returns. Stay focused, adaptable, and dedicated to continuous learning, and the world of profitable house flipping will be within your reach.

CHAPTER 6

FROM REALTOR TO REAL ESTATE INVESTOR: $97,000 IN 97 DAYS

My journey toward my first solo real estate deal culminated in a combination of the knowledge and skills I gained through five previous partnerships. This deal proved pivotal, transforming my career from a realtor and loan officer to a full-time real estate investor, while still maintaining my licenses. In this chapter, I'll share how I made an impressive $97,000 in just three months and the lessons I learned along the way.

JAMES AND THE GIANT FORECLOSURE

It all began with a phone call to a homeowner named James, who was facing impending foreclosure. Despite his challenging financial situation, it took several attempts before I finally connected with him. Initially, my intention was to offer my services as a realtor and list his property for sale to earn a standard commission.

The goal was to sell the home before foreclosure could occur. However, that process takes time, and I had to trust James's assurance that we had enough of it. Although he insisted that he was working on a loan modification, something still felt off.

Several months later, I attended the sheriff's foreclosure auction held every other Tuesday in my county. To my astonishment, James's name was called. Not only did we not have as much time as I thought, but the situation was dire. This experience underscored a crucial lesson: sellers often downplay their situations, not out of deceit but to maintain a facade of control.

Without hesitation, I rushed back to the office and called James to inform him of this unfortunate turn of events. He was devastated, and I promised to visit him to see how I could assist.

During my drive to James's condo, I contacted a friend at the sheriff's office to inquire about rescinding the sale. Although it seemed unlikely, I discovered that James had ten days to resolve the situation, known as the "Right of Redemption Period." This allowed him to repay the total amount owed, including the sheriff's fees, to reclaim ownership of the property. Armed with this new information, I met with James and his family, fully grasping the gravity of their situation.

As I sat with James, I could feel his frustration and fear. Who could blame him? He and his family were on the brink of being evicted from their home, potentially with nowhere to go. It's a horror story that plays out far too often in America.

I assured him that there was always hope and asked for his trust. Even though I didn't have a clear plan at the time, I was committed to finding a solution. Partnering was no longer my preferred option, and securing funds from traditional lenders within the ten-day timeframe seemed implausible. However, I stumbled upon an online real estate program that connected me with a local investor offering private lending.

After presenting the property's details and financial requirements, they agreed to fund $165,000 for acquisition and renovation, including a $25,000 net profit for James. This news brought immense relief and joy to him and his family, providing them *with the means to start over somewhere else and granting James some much-needed breathing room. The relief on his face when I explained the solution also lifted my own heart.*

Challenges and Triumphs

Both James and I felt we were nearing the finish line. However, the road to closing the deal was fraught with obstacles. Ten days can feel incredibly short when you're navigating the complexities of banks and real estate!

Title issues and other complications prolonged the process, pushing us to the final day of James's redemption period. With the help of my attorney, we completed the necessary paperwork and rushed the redemption check to the sheriff's office right after closing. Together, we managed to save the day. After successfully resolving these issues, I assisted James in finding a new apartment, ensuring his family had a place to call home.

Once the property was vacant, I shifted my focus to its renovation. Working with a budget of $10,000, I faced the challenge of completing necessary repairs on time. The situation was tight, and my skills were truly tested given the limited funds and extensive work required. Fortunately, I had negotiated a three-month hold on mortgage payments with the lender, giving me a two-month window before the first payment was due.

Before listing the property, I conducted a comparative market analysis and noted a significant increase in condo prices due to the newly established train station nearby. Easily accessible mass transit is always a plus, and the appeal of condo living attracts a wide range of demographics.

Taking advantage of this demand, I listed the condo for $295,000, offering a slightly higher commission to selling agents. Sometimes, incentivizing offers in response to local trends can make all the difference. By riding the wave of *demand, I hoped to achieve a favorable outcome for everyone involved.*

My strategy paid off, resulting in multiple offers as buyers vied to outbid one another. After careful consideration and a slight bidding war, I sold the property for an impressive $305,000. After accounting for commissions, closing costs, and fees from the private lender, my net profit at closing amounted to $97,000.

A Life-Altering Shift

Receiving such a substantial sum of money was a life-changing moment for my family and me. I vividly recall showing the check to my loved ones in disbelief before quickly depositing it into my account. In one fell swoop, I transitioned from rags to riches, officially establishing myself as a real estate investor.

This extraordinary experience taught me that our current circumstances do not define our future; there is always hope for something better. However, merely wishing for change isn't the wisest choice. Sometimes, to change our situation, we must change our environment. We can also be agents of change in the lives of others.

The lessons I learned from helping James and others facing foreclosure became invaluable tools for empowering home-owners to transition from victims to victors—financially, mentally, and spiritually. I discovered more than just a career path; I found my mission in life and my reason for being. I aimed to become a beacon of hope for those in need.

With this remarkable success, I embarked on a new chapter in my real estate journey, eager to explore the countless opportunities awaiting me as an investor. Little did I know that this first solo deal was just the beginning of an exciting and prosperous career in real estate.

CHAPTER 7

A NOTE TO THE WISE: BEYOND REAL ESTATE INVESTING

With the sale of James' old home, I had become a successful real estate investor. However, this journey required wearing multiple hats, and life was about to teach me that lesson in a profound way. I was soon forced to step into the role of a banker!

The idea of becoming a banker was foreign to me, something I had never considered. Yet, life has a way of surprising us. It all began when I was helping my second client avoid foreclosure. Everything seemed to be going smoothly until a troublesome line of credit on her home prevented me from purchasing it at a profitable price. That one obstacle created significant challenges, leaving me with far less money than I had anticipated.

For aspiring real estate investors, the key takeaway is this: conduct thorough due diligence on a home's title. If there are outstanding financial obligations from the previous owner, they may become your responsibility, eating into your profits. When margins are tight, this can quickly turn a promising deal into a financial disaster.

I found myself back on the block where I had sold the property to the nuns. Oakland Terrace was a charming street in a desirable neighborhood. Since selling the home to the nuns, the area had become more sought after, attracting relatively affluent buyers. To my surprise, I discovered another homeowner facing default. In a twist of fate, she sought me out, aware of my previous success with the brick beauty sold to the Catholic Church.

Initially, it almost didn't work out. While her first mortgage was a manageable $70,000, the second mortgage on the property amounted to $25,000. Given the extensive repairs needed to make the property marketable, I thought I couldn't purchase it.

Just as I was about to break the news to her, an idea struck me. "Can I get permission to speak to your second mortgage lender?" I asked. With the first mortgage already in foreclosure, the second mortgage holder stood to lose their investment. No bank wants to take a total loss, so perhaps there was a way for me to help the homeowner, the lender, and myself.

Determined to explore this opportunity, I spent hours making phone calls and navigating various bank departments. I almost gave up several times; contacting someone with real authority in a bank is never easy. Finally, after what felt like weeks of trying, I managed to reach a decision-maker at the bank.

With boldness, I faxed them an offer of $1,000 for the $25,000 note—an audacious move, or so I thought. To my astonishment, they countered with $2,000. I couldn't believe it! The bank agreed to transfer the $25,000 note and mortgage to me for just $2,000. In that instant, I became the new banker for that homeowner, stepping into the second lien holder's position. With the deal finalized, I purchased the property and began renovations.

After investing time, effort, and $50,000 in renovations, I sold the property, netting a handsome profit of around $50,000.

This experience showcased the power of creative thinking, approaching problems from new angles, and seizing opportunities that others might overlook. Here's how the numbers played out:

Math:

$70,000 (1st mortgage) + $2,000 (2nd mortgage negotiated down from $25,000) = $72,000 total debt to be paid off, compared to $95,000 if we hadn't secured the short sale on the second loan. We saved $23,000 on the total liens.

Beware of Unscrupulous Attorneys!

Working with the homeowner on Oakland Terrace was a success, a "note gone right." However, not all transactions end so positively. The real estate industry has its ups and downs for everyone involved, including investors and bankers. I want to share an example of a note gone wrong.

I learned a valuable lesson when a seller's attorney deceived me, sabotaging a deal I had negotiated down from a $100,000 first mortgage to $20,000. This experience taught me to remain cautious and skeptical of everyone, especially attorneys. Many in the real estate industry are willing to exploit others if it means advancing their own interests.

I should have learned this lesson from my previous disastrous partnership, but I expected more from an attorney. After all, aren't they supposed to act ethically and adhere to a code of conduct? Perhaps in theory, but not always in practice.

In my pursuit of abandoned houses, which often hold hidden opportunities, I stumbled upon a property in Newark, NJ. The absence of trash cans on collection day and other subtle signs indicated a vacant property, prompting me to investigate further.

Exploring the Abandoned House

As an investor, I have a knack for spotting potential in distressed properties. This particular house caught my eye because of its neglected appearance. Although the lawn was trimmed, it lacked the meticulous care evident in neighboring yards. The blinds were in disrepair, and an accumulation of junk mail confirmed my suspicion that the house was unoccupied.

Identifying abandoned homes in well-maintained neighborhoods can be challenging, but they often represent hidden opportunities for savvy investors. Determined to gather more information, I introduced myself to the neighbors, who revealed that the owner had passed away a decade ago, while his wife had relocated to Florida. The community had been maintaining the property on her behalf and expressed a strong desire for someone to purchase and renovate it.

Maintaining the property was costing the neighborhood money, and abandoned homes pose risks even in affluent areas. Once it becomes known that a home is abandoned, it attracts squatters, thieves, and vandalism, leading to a decline in surrounding property values. Clearly, it was in the community's best interest for someone to renovate and sell the home.

Tracking Down the Homeowner

Since the wife had moved away and I had no direct contact information, I conducted a skip trace to locate her. This process involves gathering details about a person and filtering them through a database. It took some effort, as she had moved several times, but eventually, I obtained her phone number and left a message.

Later that evening, she returned my call. After negotiations, we settled on a deal where I would pay her $5,000 if I could successfully negotiate down the liens on the property. However, there was a catch: she insisted that I work with her former attorney in New Jersey, citing concerns about sharing personal information over the phone. In this age of identity theft, I understood her worries, even if I wasn't thrilled about her requirement. Reluctantly, I agreed, unaware of the ordeal that lay ahead.

The Deceptive Attorney

After ordering the property title, I discovered a $100,000 first mortgage and an $80,000 tax lien attached to it. No one had paid the property taxes for over a decade, not even the bank. Once I secured permission to enter the property, I estimated that approximately $50,000 would be needed to bring it up to market standards. In that desirable neighborhood, the property could easily be valued at $250,000 post-renovation.

Considering these factors, my Maximum Allowable Offer (MAO) stood at $160,000, including the $5,000 owed to the seller. Overall, this deal seemed beneficial for everyone involved. However, when I entrusted the attorney with my offer of $10,000 to the bank, expecting his cooperation, things took an unexpected turn.

Months of Frustration

After submitting my offer to the attorney, I waited. Weeks turned into months, and my attempts to contact him became increasingly futile. Calls went unanswered, and when I visited his office, I was always told he had just stepped out or was in a meeting.

The attorney's lack of response left me frustrated. After three months, I reached my breaking point and informed the seller that I needed her to provide me with the mortgage company's contact information. Fed up with her attorney's unresponsiveness, she finally agreed.

Little did we know the shocking truth that awaited us.

Revelation and Betrayal

Upon contacting the bank directly, I inquired about my offer, only to discover that they had received a proposal from an attorney's office, but not mine. The attorney had not forwarded my proposal to the bank as expected; instead, he had submitted his own offer!

The bank, not satisfied with my initial $10,000 offer, had counter-offered at $20,000, but the attorney's office had never responded, leaving negotiations at a standstill. Disheartened but determined to move forward, I sought a way to salvage the situation. I had invested too much time and effort into this deal to walk away now, and the seller needed someone to advocate for her rights as well.

I offered to pay the bank's requested amount and sought written confirmation to proceed with the closing. However, my hopes were dashed when the banker informed me that another buyer had just wired $22,000 to purchase the note. Where had this mystery buyer come from? They had swooped in and taken the property for themselves.

It turned out the attorney had colluded with a friend to thwart both the seller and me. Of course, I didn't realize this at the time. It took considerable effort to unmask the villain behind this scheme.

Unmasking the Attorney's Scheme

The attorney's original plan had been to purchase the note for mere pennies on the dollar and then foreclose on the seller, leaving her with nothing while excluding me from the deal. However, our direct contact with the lender disrupted his scheme.

Outraged by the attorney's actions, the seller confronted him and threatened legal action. In response, he made a superficial offer of $6,000 to pacify her, surpassing my initial offer by a thousand dollars and successfully cutting me out. Although the seller wasn't thrilled, she accepted the additional money, leaving me out in the cold.

Ultimately, the attorney acquired the mortgage, leaving me powerless. The note's value exceeded $100,000, considering the principal, interest, and accumulated charges over the past decade. This ordeal marked my first encounter with a deceitful attorney, but it certainly wouldn't be the last. It did, however, alert me to the existence of unscrupulous legal practitioners, which proved to be an invaluable lesson.

The Takeaway

This unfortunate experience with the conniving attorney serves as a stark reminder to exercise caution when dealing with legal professionals. While not all attorneys are predators—many prioritize integrity—it's always best to work directly with the homeowner. This experience taught me to remain vigilant and skeptical, especially when attorneys are involved.

Note: Buying notes can be profitable. By purchasing defaulted mortgage notes from banks at a discount, investors can potentially negotiate with homeowners for a "Deed in Lieu of Foreclosure" or work towards finding an end buyer, generating substantial profits. Foreclosing on the property is also an option if necessary.

Note Buying: A Candid Exploration

Note buying is not for the faint-hearted or those lacking capital, as it typically incurs additional expenses like attorney fees, cleanup costs, security, and winterizing. Additionally, finding lenders willing to sell individual loans can be challenging, as they usually prefer to sell notes in bulk.

However, note buying offers control over the property's outcome and the potential to earn profits without taking possession of it. For example, if you purchase a $20,000 note on a property valued at $100,000 and the property sells for $60,000 at auction, you could earn a gross profit of $40,000 without acquiring the property.

That said, pursuing a deficiency judgment against the property owner for any shortfall in the note's value can involve significant legal fees, which I don't recommend. Instead, it's wiser to focus on strategies that generate profits while minimizing unnecessary legal complications.

Exploring the Note-Buying Process

Let's delve into the note-buying process. While it differs from conventional real estate investing, it can offer several advantages and opportunities. Here are some key considerations:

1. **Mitigating Risk:** When purchasing mortgage notes, investors can assess the underlying collateral—the property itself. This allows for a thorough evaluation of the property's condition, location, and potential value. Don't miss this opportunity! Use it to make informed decisions, resulting in better investments and protecting yourself from excess risk.

2. **Flexibility in Exit Strategies:** Note buying provides various exit strategies tailored to your unique needs, goals, and risk appetite. You can negotiate loan modifications, workout agreements, or offer incentives to homeowners for a successful resolution. If necessary, you can also initiate foreclosure proceedings to take control of the property.

Remember, at this stage, you technically own the loan and can act as a bank. However, avoid unethical or underhanded actions, as they can tarnish your reputation and make others less willing to work with you.

3. **Leveraging Professional Assistance:** Engaging experienced attorneys, real estate agents, and other professionals who specialize in note buying can streamline the process and increase your chances of success. These experts can provide valuable insights, handle legal aspects, and ensure compliance with local regulations, minimizing potential pitfalls. I always recommend working with experienced professionals to avoid costly mistakes and limit risks.

4. **Building Relationships with Lenders:** While purchasing individual mortgage notes can be rewarding, establishing relationships with banks and other lending institutions can grant access to larger portfolios of notes. This can open up more opportunities for acquiring multiple notes, diversifying your investments, and potentially negotiating better deals. Building relationships with lenders is easier than it seems; just reach out, get to know the people you'll be working with, and maintain contact.

5. **Expanding into Secondary Markets:** Note buying allows investors to expand their reach beyond traditional real estate markets. Consider exploring distressed markets where mortgage defaults are more common, as these often offer undervalued properties at significant discounts, leading to higher potential returns. Don't limit yourself; there are more options for success than you realize—explore them!

As with any investment strategy, thorough research, proper risk assessment, and ongoing monitoring are crucial. Staying informed about market trends, regulatory changes, and best practices in note buying is essential for optimizing success.

Note buying can be a lucrative avenue for real estate investors, providing opportunities to acquire discounted properties, exercise control over outcomes, and generate profits without ownership. But what does the process entail? If you've never dealt with a homeowner in default or negotiated with a bank, it can be daunting. Let's break it down into manageable steps.

Steps to Buy a Defaulted Mortgage Note at a Discount from a Bank:

1. Research and Identify Target Banks: Start by researching banks with a history of selling defaulted mortgage notes. Look for those with significant distressed assets or non-performing loans on their balance sheets. A bank's history of selling notes increases your chances of success, and having a substantial inventory of poor-performing notes can lead to better deals.

2. Establish Relationships: Reach out to the appropriate departments within the target banks, such as loan workout or asset management. Introduce yourself as a note investor and express your interest in purchasing defaulted mortgage notes. Building relationships with key contacts in these departments can increase your chances of receiving information about available notes. Remember, banks are more likely to work with individuals they know and have interacted with before.

3. Due Diligence: After identifying potential notes, conduct comprehensive due diligence on the underlying properties. This includes evaluating the property's condition, location, market value, outstanding liens, and any associated risks.

This is your opportunity to make an informed decision. It's

not just about finding a great deal; you must also ensure you can sell the property later. Assess the property itself, including renovation costs, and investigate the local neighborhood and market trends. Only with a complete understanding of the situation should you decide to proceed.

4. Evaluate Note Pricing: Establish the fair market value of the note by considering factors such as the outstanding loan balance, property value, and the borrower's financial situation. This assessment will enable you to negotiate a favorable purchase price with the bank.

This step is crucial and can determine the success of your deal. Overpaying could turn a profitable investment into a costly mistake. Seek assistance from local experts to ensure you make the best offer.

5. Negotiate with the Bank: Work with the bank to acquire the note at a discounted price. Present supporting evidence for your valuation and build a compelling case for why the bank should consider your offer, even if it is significantly lower than the note's value.

Supporting evidence may include estimates, data on population trends, and planned developments in the area. Local experts, such as real estate agents, property inspectors, and builders, can provide valuable insights to strengthen your negotiation.

6. Review and Sign Purchase Agreement: Once you reach an agreement with the bank, carefully review the purchase agreement. It should detail the terms of the transaction, including the purchase price, any contingencies, and closing timelines. If needed, seek legal advice to ensure the agreement protects your interests.

Remember, you don't know what you don't know. Never assume you fully understand a legal agreement, especially if you are new to the process. A trusted attorney or experienced paralegal can help you navigate these complexities.

7. Perform Legal and Title Review: Engage a qualified

attorney or title company to conduct a thorough legal and title review of the note and related documents. This step is crucial for identifying any potential issues or risks associated with the note or the underlying property.

Title problems can be time-consuming and expensive to resolve, and they may even justify walking away from a deal. Competing claims to the title can diminish your profit or complicate ownership, making it difficult to sell the property and achieve your financial goals.

8. Arrange Financing: Assess the funding required to purchase the note. If necessary, secure financing from private lenders, hard money lenders, or other sources to cover the purchase price and any associated costs.

A solid understanding of your financing options is essential. We discussed these in a previous chapter, so you should have a strategy in place. Be prepared to use multiple financing sources, especially early in your career.

9. Closing the Transaction: Once all due diligence is complete, financing is secured, and any outstanding conditions are met, proceed with the closing. Ensure all necessary documents are properly executed, and funds are transferred to finalize the purchase.

Depending on the bank's requirements, this process may be straightforward, involving the transfer of funds and signing relevant documents. However, every situation is unique, so be aware of your specific circumstances and ensure all details are correctly handled.

10. Post-Purchase Management: After acquiring the note, develop a strategy for managing the asset. This may involve working with the borrower to modify the loan, initiating foreclosure proceedings, or exploring other options to maximize returns.

Remember, you are now the bank. You own the mortgage and have various options at your disposal. Engage professionals, such as attorneys or loan servicers, if needed, to navigate the post-purchase process effectively.

Purchasing defaulted mortgage notes can be complex, requiring expertise in legal matters, negotiations, and property evaluation. Seeking guidance from experienced professionals, such as real estate attorneys or note-buying experts, can help ensure a smoother and more successful transaction.

CHAPTER 8

IDENTIFYING MOTIVATED SELLERS AND TARGETS OF OPPORTUNITY

In the realm of real estate investing, identifying motivated sellers and targets of opportunity is crucial for achieving success. Motivated sellers are individuals facing unique circumstances that prompt them to consider favorable deals. Conversely, a "target of opportunity" refers to a property rather than a seller or owner.

By understanding and pursuing these opportunities, you can maximize profitability while helping others resolve significant challenges they may face. In this chapter, we will explore various types of motivated sellers and targets of opportunity, offering strategies to help you locate and approach them effectively.

DISTRESSED SELLERS

Distressed sellers are individuals encountering financial or personal hardships that compel them to sell their properties quickly. Situations such as job losses, divorces, and family deaths can drive someone into this position. To identify distressed sellers, consider the following methods:

- **Local Real Estate Agents:** Build relationships with agents who specialize in distressed properties. They can provide access to listings and valuable leads, often before they hit the market, giving you an edge over the competition.
- **Foreclosure Listings:** Keep an eye on foreclosure listings or notices of default, which indicate properties at risk of foreclosure. Owners in this situation may be motivated to sell to avoid the negative consequences of foreclosure. Good sources for this information include local newspapers, public records, real estate agents, and real estate auctions.
- **Bank-Owned Properties:** Reach out to local banks or lending institutions to inquire about bank-owned properties, which are often sold at discounted prices. Since these properties may not be actively advertised, contacting banks directly is essential. Additionally, REO platforms like Auction.com or Xome can be useful resources.

Expired Listings

Expired listings refer to properties that were previously on the market but did not sell. To find these listings and motivated sellers, utilize the following strategies:

- **Multiple Listing Service (MLS):** Access the MLS database or collaborate with a real estate agent to obtain expired listing information. Analyze the reasons behind the property's failure to sell, such as overpricing or inadequate marketing. A property may remain unsold due to its condition, but with some sweat equity and minimal investment, the situation could change.

- **Direct Mail Campaigns:** Implement targeted direct mail campaigns directed at homeowners with recently expired listings. Craft compelling messages that express your interest in purchasing their property and offer potential solutions. Many owners are stressed and uncertain about their next steps, and you could be their lifeline.
- **Online Listing Platforms:** Regularly check online listing platforms for expired listings. Some platforms allow you to filter and search specifically for expired or withdrawn listings. Sites like Zillow and Auction.com are particularly useful, as they often feature expired listings before foreclosure.

Probate or Inherited Properties

Probate or inherited properties arise from the passing of a property owner. To locate these properties and motivated sellers, consider these methods:

- **Probate Court Records:** Search probate court records to identify properties undergoing probate. These records typically provide information about the deceased owner and the appointed executor or administrator. Many heirs are willing to sell quickly, as they may not want to assume ownership of the property.
- **Estate Attorneys:** Develop relationships with estate attorneys who handle probate cases. They can notify you of potential properties entering the market. Attorneys focusing on wills, trusts, and estate planning can provide valuable insights before properties become available to the public.

- **Public Notices:** Check local newspapers or online publications for probate notices related to inherited properties. Hyper-local publications, such as small-town newspapers or county-wide publications, are excellent resources.

ABSENTEE OWNERS

Absentee owners are individuals who own properties but do not live in the same location. They may or may not act as landlords.

Landlords who rent out properties in areas where they don't reside are technically absentee owners, but others may own a property without living in the area or renting it out. To find absentee owners and potential motivated sellers, employ the following techniques:

- **Visit the Tax Assessor's Office:** Contact your local tax assessor's office to obtain lists of properties with different mailing addresses than their physical locations. These are likely absentee-owned properties. Additionally, the office may provide information on properties with unpaid tax debt, which can be indicative of absentee ownership.
- **Use Skip Tracing Services:** Skip tracing services or professional data providers specializing in locating absentee owners can be invaluable. They utilize various data sources to find accurate contact information to connect you with absentee owners.
- **Explore DIY Options:** Conduct driving tours in target areas to identify properties that appear vacant or exhibit signs of absentee ownership. Over time, you will start recognizing the telltale signs that distinguish these properties. You can also research

property ownership records through public databases or online resources.

Upcoming Foreclosures

Properties facing impending foreclosure present valuable opportunities for connecting with motivated sellers. To identify these properties and engage with owners who need to sell, consider these tips:

- **Attend Public Foreclosure Auctions:** Locate and attend public foreclosure auctions, where properties are sold to satisfy outstanding debts. These auctions often provide insights into upcoming properties, and you can sometimes purchase properties for a fraction of their value.
- **Study Pre-Foreclosure Lists:** Access pre-foreclosure lists or services that provide information about homeowners in default on their mortgages. Contact these homeowners directly to discuss options for purchasing the property before foreclosure. You might be able to negotiate a purchase with the owner or engage with the bank to become the lienholder.
- **Search for Foreclosure Notices:** Regularly monitor public records, local newspapers, and online platforms for foreclosure notices or lis pendens filings (note that a lis pendens filing indicates that a lawsuit has been or is being filed and will affect the title). These filings signal properties at risk of foreclosure.

Vacant Houses

Vacant houses often display signs of neglect or abandonment, making them prime candidates for investment. These properties may have been inherited by family members after the original owner's death or could belong to an out-of-town owner who is no longer interested in maintaining or owning the property. To identify and track down these properties, consider the following tips:

- **Neglected Exterior**: Look for properties with overgrown grass, unkempt landscaping, broken windows, or boarded-up doors. These signs of neglect often indicate a vacant property or a situation that may lead to a quick sale.
- **Accumulation of Mail or Newspapers**: Check for a significant buildup of mail, newspapers, or packages at the property's doorstep or mailbox. When combined with neglect, this is a strong indicator that the property is vacant.
- **No Utilities or Lack of Activity**: Observe properties without visible signs of utility usage, such as lights left on at night or water running. Monitor the property over an extended period to ensure there's no activity, distinguishing between actual vacancies and homes where owners may simply be on vacation.
- **Online Property Records**: Utilize online resources like property records or local government databases to gather information about ownership and status. Pay attention to properties with out-of-state owners, unclear ownership, or tax debts.
- **Neighbor Observations**: Speak with neighbors or residents who might have information about the property's status or the owner's absence. This tactic

has proven effective for me; neighbors often know the situation of homes in their area.

- **Driving for Dollars**: Conduct driving tours around your target area, specifically looking for vacant houses. Take note of property addresses and research ownership details through public records or online databases. It may be beneficial to have someone else drive while you note the addresses and physical descriptions.

Understanding various types of motivated sellers and potential investment opportunities is essential for real estate investors. By focusing on distressed sellers, expired listings, probate or inherited properties, absentee owners, upcoming foreclosures, and vacant houses, you can increase your chances of finding lucrative investment opportunities.

Use the strategies outlined in this chapter to locate and approach motivated sellers effectively. Remember to exercise discretion, verify information, and respect privacy laws throughout the process. Be flexible in your approach; some owners may want to sell outright, while others might require you to collaborate with a lender. Always remain vigilant against unethical individuals looking to exploit the situation, and protect yourself and others involved in the transaction.

CHAPTER 9

DRESS TO IMPRESS: FIXING UP
DISTRESSED PROPERTIES

Renovating distressed properties in real estate investing can be a high-risk, high-reward endeavor. This process requires experience, problem-solving skills, and careful consideration, as well as either significant sweat equity or connections with reliable professionals (contractors and other experts).

In this chapter, we will explore the challenges and potential rewards of renovating properties, sharing insights from real-life experiences and practical advice to help you navigate this aspect of real estate investing. Additionally, I will outline a step-by-step system for rehabbing residential single-family houses based on industry best practices.

1. ASSESSING PROPERTY VIABILITY

Before starting any renovation project, evaluate whether the property is worth renovating. This is a crucial "make or break" point; some properties are worth rehabbing, while others are not. Follow these steps:

Conduct a Financial Analysis:

- Estimate potential renovation costs, including materials, labor, and permits.
- Research the market value of renovated properties in the area to gauge the post-renovation value.
- Analyze potential profit margins by subtracting total renovation costs from the estimated post-renovation value.

Conduct a Risk Assessment:

- Thoroughly inspect the property for structural issues, major repairs, or environmental concerns such as asbestos or mold.
- Evaluate how these issues might impact the project timeline and budget.
- Decide whether the potential profit outweighs the associated risks and whether to proceed with the renovation.

Consider Alternative Strategies:

- Assess market demand and potential profit margins for selling the property "as is" to another buyer.
- Compare the financial implications and time commitments of renovating versus selling the property without renovations.
- Make an informed decision about whether to proceed with the renovation or pursue an alternative strategy.

2. DEVELOPING A DETAILED RENOVATION PLAN

Once you've confirmed the property is viable for renovation, create a detailed plan to guide the process, including the following steps:

Scope of Work:

- Identify the specific areas and components of the house that require renovation. Classify them as "must renovate" and "nice to renovate," focusing on the must-haves first.
- Determine the level of renovation needed, whether it's a cosmetic update or a full-scale overhaul, directly linking this to your list of must-haves versus nice-to-haves.
- Create a comprehensive list of necessary repairs, replacements, and upgrades. This will inform your budget and timeline.

Budgeting

- Estimate costs for materials, labor, permits, and any additional expenses using current pricing rather than historical figures.
- Create a budget spreadsheet that details each renovation item and its associated cost.
- Allocate contingency funds to cover unexpected expenses or changes in scope. Always prepare for the unexpected.

Timelines and Scheduling

- Establish a realistic timeline for completing each step of the renovation process. Your time estimates will improve with experience.
- Consider dependencies between tasks and create a schedule that optimizes efficiency while respecting these dependencies.

- Communicate the timeline to contractors, suppliers, and other team members to ensure everyone is aligned.

HIRING CONTRACTORS AND MANAGING THE RENOVATION

The success of your renovation project relies heavily on your choice of contractors. Hire skilled and ethical professionals who prioritize quality without necessarily being the most expensive. Shop around, compare options, read reviews, and speak with previous clients.

Contractor Selection:

- Seek recommendations from trusted sources, such as other investors or real estate professionals.
- Interview multiple contractors and obtain detailed bids. Ensure you are making fair comparisons.
- Evaluate contractors based on professionalism, track record, and their ability to deliver quality work within the agreed timeline and budget.

Contracts and Agreements:

- Create a comprehensive contract that outlines the scope of work, payment terms, and project milestones.
- Include penalty clauses for delays or unsatisfactory workmanship to protect your investment.
- Clearly communicate expectations, ensuring both parties understand the terms and conditions. It's

crucial that contractors know what you expect and when.

Project Management:

- Regularly communicate with the contractor to monitor progress and address any issues promptly. Inadequate communication can lead to delays and complications.
- Maintain an organized system for tracking expenses, invoices, and permits, as these impact both costs and timelines.
- Conduct periodic site visits to ensure the renovation is progressing as planned. Active involvement is key for a successful investor.

QUALITY CONTROL AND FINISHING TOUCHES

The final steps of any renovation project are as critical as the initial phases. This is when you ensure everything is in order before listing the property for sale.

Inspections:

- Schedule necessary inspections to ensure compliance with local building codes and regulations.
- Address any issues identified during inspections promptly to maintain project momentum.

Attention to Detail:

- Focus on final touches that enhance the property's

appeal and market value, such as exterior painting
and landscaping.

- Install high-quality fixtures, flooring, and finishes
  that cater to the preferences of your target market.
- Consider staging the property to highlight its
  potential to prospective buyers. Lightly staged homes
  often sell faster than empty ones.

Final Walkthrough:

- Conduct a thorough inspection of the completed
  renovation before listing the property for sale. Be
  critical to catch any issues before buyers do.
- Resolve any outstanding problems or deficiencies to
  present a fully renovated and move-in-ready home.
  Including a clause in your contractor agreements to
  ensure this is advisable.

Renovating distressed residential properties can be profitable
with a systematic and well-planned approach. By assessing property viability, developing a detailed renovation plan, hiring reliable contractors, and ensuring quality control throughout the
process, you can transform dilapidated houses into attractive
homes.

Always consider financial analysis, risk assessment, and
alternative strategies when deciding to undertake a renovation
project. With experience and a step-by-step system, you can
successfully navigate the challenges of rehabbing houses and
thrive as an investor.

CHAPTER 10

SELLING RENOVATED HOUSES

Selling a renovated house marks the pinnacle of a successful real estate investment. However, you can't rely on the property to sell itself; you must actively enhance its appeal to your target audience.

To ensure a smooth selling process and maximize your profit, it's essential to adopt best practices from top realtors and experienced house flippers. In this chapter, we will explore key strategies for selling renovated houses, drawing on insights from industry experts. We will focus on offering value, effective staging techniques, and marketing strategies.

1. OFFERING VALUE

A fundamental principle highlighted by top realtors and house flippers is the importance of providing value to potential buyers. Buyers seek a blend of financial savings and quality features throughout the property. Consider the following best practices:

· · ·

Quality Renovations

- **Prioritize High-Quality Upgrades:** Focus on premium renovations that distinguish your home from the competition. Opt for features like wainscoting and crown molding instead of just fresh paint and minor touch-ups.
- **Hire Skilled Contractors:** Engaging experienced craftsmen ensures that your renovations are executed to a high standard. Professional workmanship can make a significant difference in the overall appeal.
- **Attention to Detail:** Use high-quality materials, modern fixtures, and energy-efficient upgrades. Elements such as real wood, durable metals, and textured finishes can enhance both the property's attractiveness and its value.

Pricing Strategy

- **Consult a Knowledgeable Real Estate Agent:** Work with an experienced realtor to establish an optimal listing price. I recommend getting a professional appraisal unless your agent has a strong grasp of the market.
- **Conduct Market Research:** Analyze comparable sales and current market demand to determine a competitive price that attracts the right buyers and expedites the sale.
- **Set a Realistic Price:** Establish a competitive price that reflects the added value from your renovations. Avoid pricing too high or too low; aim for the "Goldilocks" zone, recognizing that your home may not appeal to every buyer. Focus on what your target

audience is willing to pay for the quality renovations you've made.

Highlighting Features

- **Accentuate Key Features:** Identify and showcase the most appealing aspects of your renovated home, such as spacious lots or central locations. Use these features as the foundation of your property description to help buyers envision themselves in the space.
- **Emphasize Unique Selling Points:** Highlight distinctive features like a stunning kitchen, luxurious bathroom, or enhanced curb appeal. These elements should not only appeal to buyers but also differentiate your property from others on the market.
- **Craft Engaging Listings:** Use captivating descriptions, professional photography, and virtual tours to convey the value of these features. Your property description should tell a story that illustrates life in the home and what buyers can expect.

2. STAGING TECHNIQUES

Successful realtors and house flippers understand the importance of staging in creating a compelling environment for potential buyers. Staging goes beyond merely furnishing a home; it involves adding enough elements to connect with buyers emotionally. Here are some effective practices:

Depersonalization and Decluttering

- **Remove Personal Items:** Clear out personal belongings, family photos, and excessive clutter to foster a neutral and inviting atmosphere. While some furnishings are necessary, aim for a clean, blank canvas that allows buyers to envision themselves in the space.
- **Create a Neutral Palette:** Present a clean environment that emphasizes key features of the home while aligning with its architectural style. Avoid overly bold decor that might distract potential buyers.

Furniture and Decor

- **Use Tasteful Arrangements:** Arrange furniture and decor stylishly to enhance each room's visual appeal. Think of your staging as lightly sketching the character of the space, rather than fully painting it.
- **Highlight Functionality:** Showcase the potential uses of each space to inspire buyers' imaginations. For example, a long, narrow room could serve as a home office and library, while a sunroom could become a peaceful retreat.

Lighting and Ambiance

- **Maximize Natural Light:** Open curtains and blinds to create a bright, welcoming atmosphere. If necessary, consider replacing heavy or dated window treatments in key rooms with lighter options like sheers and stylish curtains that can be reused across different properties.
- **Enhance with Artificial Lighting:** Use well-placed artificial lighting to accentuate the home's best

features. Good lighting can transform small, dark areas into cozy nooks and make larger rooms feel airy and spacious.

EFFECTIVE MARKETING

If potential buyers don't know a home is for sale, they won't buy it. Therefore, effective marketing is crucial for spreading the word and showcasing the property's value. The right marketing strategy can significantly ease the selling process by conveying the home's worth to interested buyers. If you're worried about lacking experience, don't be; it's simpler than you might think. Here are some best practices to consider:

Professional Photography and Virtual Tours:

- Invest in high-quality photography to capture the essence of your renovated home. While a decent smartphone can do a lot, don't hesitate to hire a professional photographer, especially for high-value properties.
- Consider creating virtual tours or 3D walkthroughs to provide an immersive online experience. These tools allow potential buyers to explore the home without physically visiting, which is increasingly important as many buyers now seek walkthrough videos on online listing platforms.

Compelling Listing Descriptions:

- Craft engaging and informative listing descriptions that highlight the property's unique features and renovations. Be sure to mention updates, special characteristics, proximity to popular destinations, and other key selling points.
- Use descriptive language to create an emotional connection with potential buyers. Your goal is to help them envision living in the home, so your wording should reflect that aspirational experience.

Targeted Advertising:

- Utilize online platforms, social media, and local real estate networks to effectively reach your target market. Don't restrict yourself to real estate websites; platforms like Facebook offer immense marketing opportunities through posts, groups, and more.
- Consider running targeted advertising campaigns to maximize your exposure to interested buyers. Most social media platforms provide tools to fine-tune your marketing efforts based on specific demographics, ensuring that your ads remain relevant and cost-effective.

Open Houses and Showings:

- Organize well-planned open houses and showings, allowing potential buyers to experience the renovated home firsthand. These events provide a pressure-free environment for buyers, whether they come alone or with their realtors.
- Foster a warm and welcoming atmosphere during showings to help buyers envision themselves living in the space. This ties back to staging; aim for inviting

spaces that are neutral and not tied to the seller's
personal style.

By adopting the best practices from successful realtors and
experienced house flippers, you can enhance your selling experience, increase the sale price, and reduce the time your home
spends on the market. Remember, your goal is to create an irre-
sistible package that stands out and captures buyers' attention,
allowing them to imagine themselves in the home.

CHAPTER 11

FINDING PRIVATE MONEY TO FUND YOUR HOUSE FLIPS

In the world of real estate investing, securing capital is crucial. Without money, progress is limited. However, obtaining funds can be challenging, especially if you're starting out alone and lack deep pockets or direct connections to wealthy individuals.

As I mentioned in a previous chapter, conventional financing from banks and credit unions is often not viable for real estate investors. Most institutional lenders are hesitant to work with them due to perceived risks. However, private money lenders operate differently.

In this chapter, I'll explore private lending more thoroughly, discussing strategies to find private money and how to build relationships with potential lenders.

UNDERSTANDING PRIVATE MONEY LENDING

You may be somewhat familiar with the conventional lending process, which involves approaching a bank, filling out a loan application, providing financial information, and awaiting approval. Private lending is a different ballgame.

Private money lending entails obtaining funds from individuals or private institutions rather than traditional financial entities. Private lenders tend to be more flexible, offering faster approvals and customized loan terms. While your creditworthiness matters, the primary focus is on the asset's value (the home) and its potential for a quick return for the lender.

To summarize, private lenders provide:

- A faster, more reliable route to funding
- Higher interest rates
- Better approval odds
- Greater flexibility

You might be wondering, "Where do I find these lenders, and how can I convince them to lend me money?" Based on my experience, I have several recommendations.

NETWORKING WITHIN REAL ESTATE CIRCLES

Networking is a powerful way to locate private money lenders. Real estate professionals (brokers, realtors, etc.) are often well-connected in the industry. Building relationships with them can offer benefits beyond potential lenders, such as access to high-demand homes before they hit the market, trusted appraisers and surveyors, contractors, and more.

To connect with these individuals, consider the following options:

Real Estate Investment Clubs:

- Attend local real estate investment clubs and networking events to meet potential private lenders. These gatherings provide opportunities to connect with individuals interested in collaborating, especially if you already have a property in mind.

- Actively participate in discussions, share your expertise, and cultivate trust and credibility. Building genuine relationships is key; don't expect immediate acceptance if you haven't invested time in becoming part of the community. Focus on forming authentic connections, engaging in meaningful conversations, and offering insight and value first.

Real Estate Associations and Conferences

- **Join Real Estate Associations**: Connect with like-minded professionals by joining real estate associations and attending conferences. While the National Association of Realtors is well-known, each state and many cities have their own associations. My advice is to start local and gradually expand as you gain experience and respect. The same applies to real estate conferences; there are national, regional, and local events where you can meet potential lenders.
- **Networking Opportunities**: Take advantage of networking opportunities and engage in conversations about private lending. Don't overlook individuals who aren't lenders; they may still offer valuable connections. It's about who you know, and many industry professionals are connected to a wider network than you might be. Engage in discussions, build relationships, and remember that fostering connections is as crucial as finding funding.

Real Estate Professionals

- **Build Relationships**: Establish connections with real estate agents, brokers, and attorneys who work with investors. You'll encounter these professionals at the associations and conferences mentioned earlier, but don't limit your efforts to just those events. Attend local open houses, visit brokerages, and get to know real estate attorneys in your area.
- **Leverage Their Connections**: These professionals often have connections to private lenders or know individuals interested in financing real estate projects. Your success often hinges on these relationships; many successful projects arise because someone you know is connected to a potential lender.

Tap into Personal and Professional Networks

- **Utilize Your Network**: Don't think that only real estate professionals can connect you with private lenders. Friends, family, and acquaintances might have the connections or funding you need. Consider these personal and professional networks as valuable resources for private money lending.
- **Approach Individuals**: Reach out to individuals in your personal network who may be interested in real estate investment, including family, friends, and acquaintances. You may find one person willing to fund your next purchase or several individuals wanting to collaborate. Funding doesn't have to come from a single lender; multiple partners can pool resources.
- **Present Your Plans Clearly**: Clearly communicate your investment plans, demonstrate your expertise, and offer attractive terms to potential lenders. After building relationships, it's time to lay the groundwork

for a deal. Avoid empty promises; instead, showcase facts, strategies, and concrete plans that reflect your experience and thorough preparation.

- **Reach Out to Business Contacts**: Contact business associates, such as colleagues or entrepreneurs with surplus capital for investment. Former coworkers, managers, and bosses can also be worthwhile partners. Your preexisting professional relationships can make discussions smoother, as they already know your character.
- **Highlight Benefits**: Emphasize the potential benefits of real estate investing and explain how their investment can yield attractive returns. While it's important to pitch your opportunity effectively, avoid overselling. Maintain your credibility by being upfront and transparent, and never pressure someone who expresses disinterest.

ONLINE PLATFORMS AND CROWDFUNDING

- **Explore Digital Opportunities**: The digital landscape has transformed how loans are obtained. For consumers, securing a real estate loan is quick and straightforward, but real estate investors also benefit from online platforms connecting them with private lenders.
- **Peer-to-Peer Lending**: Utilize peer-to-peer lending platforms that connect borrowers with individual lenders, such as Prosper, Funding Circle, Kiva, Fundrise, and PeerStreet. Each platform has its pros and cons, so do your research before making a decision.
- **Create a Compelling Profile**: Develop a profile detailing your investment strategy, experience, and

potential returns to attract private lenders. Approach this profile like a pitch to a coworker or former boss —be authentic and transparent while making a compelling case for why your property is a suitable investment.

- **Real Estate Crowdfunding**: Consider real estate crowdfunding platforms, which allow multiple investors to contribute funds to specific projects. Examples include CrowdStreet, RealtyMogul, and Arrived.

- **Document Your Proposals**: Prepare well-documented project proposals tailored to potential investors on these platforms. Create a master proposal but be ready to customize your information for different audiences, as each lender may have varying risk tolerances and preferences.

Building Trust and Credibility

- **Establish Credibility**: Trust and credibility are essential; without them, lenders won't consider working with you. Building this trust can be challenging, but following these steps can help demonstrate your integrity.

- **Develop a Professional Business Plan**: Create a comprehensive business plan outlining your investment strategy, market analysis, and projected returns. Although drafting a business plan may require time and possibly financial resources, the investment is worthwhile. A well-researched plan shows you are informed and prepared for any eventualities.

- **Highlight Your Experience**: Showcase your experience, track record, and successful past projects to instill confidence in potential lenders. Building credibility often hinges on being perceived as an expert, even if you have completed only one or two projects. Experience in real estate or related fields also enhances your trustworthiness.

Chapter 12

Asset Protection

The Rich Don't Own, They Control

One key strategy the wealthy use to protect their assets is the principle of control without ownership. Rather than directly owning properties and assets, they utilize legal entities such as trusts and corporations to maintain control. This approach shields their assets from potential lawsuits, creditors, and even taxes.

Scenario:

Consider a successful entrepreneur named Sarah who owns multiple properties and businesses. Instead of holding these assets in her name, she places them in various trusts and LLCs. When someone attempts to sue her, they find it challenging to target her assets directly because these are legally owned by the entities, not Sarah herself.

Real-Life Example:

John D. Rockefeller, one of the wealthiest individuals in

history, famously said, "Own nothing, control everything." He employed a complex network of trusts and holding companies to control his vast empire while minimizing personal liability and taxes. By doing this, Rockefeller was able to safeguard his wealth from potential creditors and legal challenges.

Land Trusts

A land trust is a legal entity that holds ownership of real estate property. The true owner (beneficiary) remains anonymous while retaining control through a trustee. This setup offers several benefits:

- **Privacy:** Your name does not appear in public records as the owner.
- **Protection:** It becomes more difficult for potential litigants to find and seize your assets.
- **Control:** You maintain control over the property without direct ownership.

Scenario:

Consider Emily, who owns several rental properties. She places each property into a separate land trust. If a tenant attempts to sue her for an accident on one of her properties, they cannot easily discover the others she owns because they are all held in separate trusts. This anonymity reduces the likelihood of Emily being targeted personally. To learn more about trust documents, download the SMART APP at www.smartsuperapp.com to create your own.

· · ·

Real-Life Example:

Walt Disney used a land trust to acquire the land for Disneyland in Florida. By utilizing a land trust, Disney kept his identity and intentions secret, allowing him to purchase the land at lower prices than if sellers had known who was buying.

Hiding Your Assets: Avoiding Lawsuits, Liens, and Levies

By placing assets into trusts and other legal entities, you create a layer of separation between yourself and your assets. This separation helps protect your assets from lawsuits and creditors. Consider the following strategies:

- **Use Multiple Entities:** Distribute assets across different trusts and corporations to minimize risk.
- **Regular Reviews:** Periodically assess your asset protection strategies to ensure their effectiveness and compliance with current laws.

Scenario:

Michael, a physician concerned about potential malpractice lawsuits, transfers his investments and savings into a series of trusts and LLCs. This way, if he is sued, his personal assets are protected, and only the assets within his practice can be targeted.

Real-Life Example:

The Kennedy family has utilized a series of trusts and foundations to protect and manage their wealth across generations. This strategy has allowed them to preserve their fortune while minimizing exposure to lawsuits and taxes.

Probate is the legal process through which a deceased person's estate is distributed. This process can be time-consuming, costly, and public. To avoid probate:

- **Living Trusts:** Transfer assets into a living trust. Upon death, these assets pass directly to beneficiaries without going through probate.
- **Joint Ownership:** Hold property jointly with rights of survivorship. This arrangement ensures that upon death, the surviving owner automatically gains full ownership.

Scenario

Linda wants to ensure that her children inherit her home without going through probate. She transfers the house into a living trust and names her children as beneficiaries. When she passes away, the house automatically transfers to her children, avoiding the need for probate.

Real-Life Example

Actor James Dean's estate went through probate, causing delays and extra expenses. In contrast, comedian Robin Williams established trusts to ensure his estate would be distributed quickly and privately to his beneficiaries.

LLCs and Corporations

Limited Liability Companies (LLCs) and corporations provide a strong structure for protecting personal assets from business liabilities. Key benefits include:

- **Liability Protection**: Personal assets are safeguarded from business-related lawsuits and debts.
- **Tax Flexibility**: LLCs allow for flexible taxation options, potentially reducing tax liabilities.
- **Professionalism**: Operating as an LLC or corporation can enhance credibility with customers and clients.

Scenario

Tom, a freelance graphic designer, decides to form an LLC for his business. This ensures that if a client ever sues him, only the assets of the LLC are at risk, protecting his personal savings and property.

Real-Life Example

Apple Inc. began as a small business in a garage. By incorporating, Steve Jobs and Steve Wozniak shielded their personal assets from the business's liabilities, enabling them to take risks and grow the company into the tech giant it is today.

REDUCING TAXABLE INCOME: ITEMIZATIONS, DEDUCTIONS, DEPRECIATION

Tax planning is essential for asset protection. By strategically managing taxable income through itemizations, deductions, and depreciation, you can significantly reduce tax liabilities. Key strategies include:

- **Itemizing Deductions**: Carefully tracking and

claiming allowable expenses, such as mortgage
interest, property taxes, and charitable donations.

- **Depreciation**: Utilizing depreciation on property and
assets to lower taxable income.

- **Tax-Advantaged Accounts**: Using retirement
accounts and other tax-advantaged vehicles to defer
or reduce taxes.

Scenario

Karen owns a small business and invests in real estate. By
meticulously itemizing her deductions and claiming depreciation
on her properties, she significantly reduces her taxable income
each year, freeing up more money for reinvestment.

Real-Life Example

During the 2016 Presidential debate between Hillary Clinton
and Donald Trump, the discussion highlighted how the wealthy
exploit the tax code to minimize their federal taxes. Former Pres-
ident Donald Trump boasted about using tax write-offs and
depreciation to lower his taxable income. When Hillary Clinton
pointed out that Trump paid zero in federal income taxes, he
replied, "That's what makes me smart!"

Asset protection involves more than just shielding wealth
from lawsuits and creditors; it requires strategic planning for
long-term financial security. By understanding and implementing
these strategies—controlling rather than owning, utilizing land
trusts, avoiding probate, leveraging LLCs and corporations, and
optimizing tax liabilities—you can effectively protect and grow
your wealth.

Implementing these techniques requires careful planning and
professional guidance. The benefits in terms of financial security
and peace of mind are well worth the effort. By taking a proac-

tive approach to asset protection, you can ensure that your hard-earned wealth is safeguarded for future generations.

"Raggedy Riches: How I Got Rich from Raggedy Houses" has taken you on a journey through the world of real estate investing, specifically focusing on the fix-and-flip strategy. Throughout this book, we explored four essential steps: Find It, Fund It, Fix It, and Flip It. We discussed the challenges of identifying profitable properties, securing funding from various sources, executing successful renovations, and ultimately reaping the rewards of a well-executed flip.

As you reach the end of this book, I hope you have gained valuable insights and practical knowledge to empower your real estate investing journey. Whether you are a seasoned investor or just starting out, the key takeaways from "Raggedy Riches" serve as guiding principles for your success.

First, diligence is critical in your property search. Develop a keen eye for identifying potential gems among raggedy houses. Look beyond surface flaws and envision the true potential within each property. Trust your instincts and conduct thorough due diligence to ensure smart investments.

Next, understand the importance of strategic financing. Explore the various funding options available, from traditional lenders to private investors. Build relationships, establish trust, and present your investment opportunities clearly and compellingly. Remember, the right financing can make or break a deal, so be persistent and think creatively.

During the renovation phase, embrace both the art and science of transforming raggedy houses into desirable homes. Surround yourself with expert contractors and professionals who share your vision and commitment to quality. Plan meticulously, set realistic timelines, and be prepared for unexpected challenges —they will occur. Each renovation project is an opportunity to refine your skills and learn from both successes and setbacks.

Finally, the culmination of your efforts lies in the flip—the moment when you turn your investment into a profitable return. Develop a comprehensive marketing strategy to attract potential buyers and showcase the true value you have created. From professional staging to effective online marketing, utilize every tool at your disposal to maximize your property's appeal. Remember, patience and perseverance are crucial during the selling process.

Conclusion

As you embark on your journey, keep in mind that success is not guaranteed. It requires dedication, continuous learning, and the ability to adapt to changing market dynamics. Embrace the lessons learned from the raggedy houses that have shaped your path and let them remind you of the resilience and tenacity required to achieve true wealth in this industry.

"Raggedy Riches" is more than just a book; it's a roadmap to financial freedom through real estate. I encourage you to take action, embrace challenges, and create your own success story. The world of real estate investing awaits you, ready to reward those bold enough to turn raggedy houses into riches.

As I conclude this book, after 11 years of toil and 23 years in the business, I'm ready for a new level in my life, and I hope you are ready for a new level in yours. See you at the top!

To learn more about how to get rich from raggedy houses, upcoming seminars, workshops, and potential business opportunities, visit www.revelopers.com, www.realestateinvestorsassociation.org, and www.njreia.com.

To learn more about trust documents, download the SMART app: https://smartsuper.app/

(Legal disclaimer: We at Revelopers, Smart Inc, Smart app its affiliates and or assignees, are not attorneys and do not provide legal advice. All content in this book is for entertainment purposes only and reflects my experience with trust documents and other techniques. Consult an attorney when creating and using legal documents. We do not provide legal or business advice of any kind throughout this book, and this extends to any affiliates or companies associated with this book.)